99947

D1476991

HERZOG & DE MEURON + AI WEIWEI
SERPENTINE GALLERY PAVILION 2012

Serpentine Gallery | Koenig Books

SERPENTINE GALLERY

SERPENTINE GALLERY

SERPENTINE GALLERY

SERPENTINE GALLERY

Contents

Sponsors' Forewords

We are delighted to be able to support the Serpentine Gallery's Pavilion commission in 2012. For the last eleven years, the Serpentine Gallery has hosted this unique commission, which is now one of the world's most visited exhibitions of architecture. It seems appropriate in this Olympic year that the designers should be Herzog & de Meuron and Ai Weiwei, given that they were the designers of the visionary 'Bird's Nest' National Stadium in Beijing for the 2008 Olympic and Paralympic Games, and appropriate as well that in this twelfth year, the design should feature 'design memories' of the previous eleven commissions. We hope that you will enjoy your visit.

Usha and Lakshmi N. Mittal
Principal Supporters of the Serpentine Gallery Pavilion 2012

Hiscox is very proud to be associated with Herzog & de Meuron and Ai Weiwei, two icons in their fields. All are leaders in contemporary creativity, and Ai Weiwei has been courageous in standing by his beliefs and artistic integrity. We are also very happy to be able to support the Serpentine Gallery again as a beacon of education and a space for fascinating and always stimulating art.

Robert Hiscox
Chairman, Hiscox
Principal Sponsor of the Serpentine Gallery Pavilion 2012

Directors' Foreword

The twelfth commission in the Serpentine Gallery's annual Pavilion series has been designed jointly by Herzog & de Meuron and Ai Weiwei. It presents an elegant, innovative and conceptually engaged approach to both the Pavilion brief and to the history of the series overall. Herzog & de Meuron and Ai Weiwei have a long-term and fruitful collaborative relationship, yet this is the first time this design team has built a structure in the UK. Their previous buildings include the acclaimed National Stadium in Beijing, also known as the 'Bird's Nest', built for the 2008 Olympic Games and winner of the RIBA Lubetkin Prize. The Pavilion that they have created for the Serpentine is presented as part of the London 2012 Festival, the culmination of the Cultural Olympiad.

Herzog & de Meuron have designed a wide range of projects to very great acclaim, from the small scale of a private home to the largest scale of urban design. Their practice has been awarded numerous prizes including the Pritzker Architecture Prize in 2001, as well as the RIBA Royal Gold Medal and Praemium Imperiale, both in 2007.

Ai Weiwei, an artist, poet and architect, is well-known globally as one of the most articulate and important critics and chroniclers of contemporary China. He has a longstanding engagement with architecture, founding the Beijing-based architecture studio FAKE Design in 2003. His work in this field began in 1999 after designing and building his own home and studios in Caochangdi on the outskirts of Beijing, and he has since designed over 60 building projects, as well as bringing many international architects to China. The 2012 Pavilion is the latest project in his ongoing relationship with the Serpentine Gallery; firstly as a participant in the *China Power Station* exhibition in 2006 and then in the *Map Marathon* in 2010.

The Serpentine's annual programme of architectural commissions was inaugurated in 2000 and Jacques Herzog, Pierre de Meuron and Ai Weiwei have taken a distinctly direct approach to the designs of their predecessors. In contrast to the frequent tendency to build upwards, or to monumentalise the space, their Pavilion plunges its visitors beneath the lawn, revealing the ghostly traces of the varied structures of the past eleven years.

Resembling an archaeological site, the Pavilion's low roof floats 1.5 metres above the grass of the park. A low plane covered in water, the steel expanse reflects the sky and its surroundings, whilst concealing below the earthy landscape formed by the architects' excavations. The designers have reconstructed the physical remains of each of the eleven Pavilions built between 2000 and 2011. These foundations have been overlaid to form a complex pattern of contours and planes, offering a terrain within which visitors can sit, walk, stand and meet.

Herzog & de Meuron and Ai Weiwei's Pavilion is a structure that bears witness to historical memory and, in that sense, it forms what historian Eric Hobsbawm once referred to as 'a protest against forgetting'. Its archaeological architecture reminds us that successful architecture is always a question of the utmost sensitivity to the site.

Acknowledging the impressive achievements of the past architects, Herzog & de Meuron and Ai Weiwei have extruded columns from the foundations of each past Pavilion, employing them as load-bearers for their roof structure. Eleven columns represent each of the previous Pavilions. The twelfth – Herzog & de Meuron and Ai Weiwei's own contribution – sits among them, an integral part of the continuing lineage of this commission.

In accordance with the collaborative practice of Herzog & de Meuron and Ai Weiwei, this Pavilion has been built to invoke the contemplation of things less visible. Presenting an impression of the structures that have gone before, this hollowed out space mines and re-examines the history of the Pavilion commissions, the park, and the city in which it sits. What is more, this unusual concave form also represents the desire of the architects to confront, or sidestep, the apparently inevitable requirement of architecture to create an object or a concrete shape.

In challenging the preconceptions of what a built structure might be, this Pavilion speaks to the Serpentine Gallery's ambition to present constructions that stretch the boundaries of contemporary architectural practice. The Pavilion programme offers audiences the opportunity to engage with the work of world-renowned architects firsthand. Exploring the potential for commissioning architecture, the Serpentine Gallery adopts an alternative approach, one that offers an immediate process for the designers involved. Working in close collaboration with a team of specialists to realise the architect's vision for the project, the timeframe is only six months from invitation to completion.

The series is unique worldwide and presents the work of an international architect or designer who has not completed a building in England at the time of the Gallery's invitation. The process of selecting the architects is guided by similar criteria used for selecting artists: it is led by the core curatorial thinking of the Gallery. Since the series began in 2000, it has realised commissions by some of the world's leading architects: Peter Zumthor, 2011; Jean Nouvel, 2010; Kazuyo Sejima and Ryue Nishizawa / SANAA, 2009; Frank Gehry, 2008; Olafur Eliasson and Kjetil Thorsen, 2007; Rem Koolhaas and Cecil Balmond, with Arup, 2006; Álvaro Siza and Eduardo Souto de Moura with Cecil Balmond – Arup, 2005; MVRDV with Arup, 2004 (unrealised); Oscar Niemeyer, 2003; Toyo Ito and Cecil Balmond, with Arup, 2002; Daniel Libeskind with Arup, 2001; and Zaha Hadid, 2000. The immediacy of the Serpentine Pavilion commission continues to provide an unparalleled site for architectural experimentation.

Each Pavilion is sited on the Gallery's lawn for the summer months, operating as a public space and as a venue the Serpentine's *Park Nights* programme. This is a series of public talks, film screenings and performances which runs from June to October, culminating with the *Serpentine Gallery Marathon*, a two-day event, the theme of which is inspired by the Serpentine Gallery Pavilion. In 2012, the *Memory Marathon* (the seventh in the series), brings together over fifty poets, writers, artists, architects, performers, musicians and other leading figures in contemporary culture to explore memory, archaeology and history through the connections between artistic and scientific enquiry.

The eleven previous Pavilion commissions have created relationships across time and space, forming a palimpsest of architectural forms beneath the grass of Kensington Gardens, a site that has been worked and reworked by many great contemporary architects. The Pavilion of Herzog & de Meuron and Ai Weiwei aims to recover memories, and following on from this, the 2012 *Marathon* will continue to question what lies beneath to uncover the traces of the lost or hidden. As the scientist Israel Rosenfield has noted, 'memory is relationship; on the one hand our temporal relationships and on the other our spatial relationships.' This year's *Marathon* will approach memory as an active practice that can question received ideas - a probing of the old in the name of the new.

The vision of the three designers of the 2012 Pavilion reflects an innovative and collaborative working practice, mirroring the dynamic history of the Pavilion commission. We are enormously grateful to Jacques Herzog, Pierre de Meuron and Ai Weiwei for accepting our invitation to design this year's Pavilion. Additionally, we are indebted to them for producing a series of Limited Editions, which are being sold in support of the project.

We would also like to acknowledge the architects' teams and collaborators. At Herzog & de Meuron, we extend our sincere thanks to Ben Duckworth and Christoph Zeller, Project Architects, whose hard work and commitment were invaluable throughout, as well as Liam Ashmore, Aliénor de Chambrier, Martin Eriksson, Mai Komuro, Donald Mak, Martin Nässén, John O'Mara, Wim Walschap and Esther Zumsteg for devoting their time and energy to the project. At Ai Weiwei's studio, E-Shyh Wong and Inserk Yang provided essential support at key stages of the project and we remain very thankful to them.

There is no budget for the Serpentine Gallery Pavilion commission. It is paid for by sponsorship help-in-kind and the sale of the finished structure, which does not cover more than 40% of its cost. The Serpentine Gallery collaborates with a group of forward-thinking companies and individuals, whose support and dedication make it possible to realise the Pavilion.

As principal supporters of the project, Usha and Lakshmi N. Mittal have played a vital role in the realisation of the Serpentine Gallery Pavilion 2012. They are ongoing patrons of the arts and architecture, and have sponsored this year's Pavilion as well as purchasing it for their collection. We extend our deepest thanks for this generosity.

We are delighted that Hiscox are sponsoring this year's Pavilion. Without their financial investment the scheme simply would not be possible. We are most grateful to Robert Hiscox, Chairman, and Steve Langan, UK Managing Director, both of whom are longstanding and valued supporters of the Serpentine.

The support of leading cork manufacturers Amorim has been fundamental to the success of this project and we would like to thank António Rios de Amorim, Chairman, Cristina Amorim, Managing Director, and Carlos de Jesus, Director of Marketing and Communication, for their generous and enthusiastic engagement with this year's Pavilion.

We are also appreciative of ESPA's support. Sue Harmsworth, CEO and Founder, and Charlie Harmsworth, Brand Director, deserve acknowledgement for their commitment towards this project.

The team at Arup has been an invaluable partner to the Serpentine Gallery for the Pavilion series, providing a range of technical, design, creative and management skills. We are thankful to Stuart Smith and Chris Neighbour for their commitment to the scheme, and also to Francesco Anselmo, Mark Freeman, Lidia Johnson, Jeff Shaw and Jack Wilshaw for giving so much of their time and energy in the development of the project. The wider Arup team have also played an important role.

RISE is a key supporter of the Pavilion programme and we are delighted to have their project and construction management expertise guiding the project. Our thanks go to Gareth Stapleton and Tom Redhouse for making this year's Pavilion a success.

Weil, Gotshal & Manges are an important partner to the Gallery throughout the year and have, once again, been essential to the Pavilion. In particular, Marco Compagnoni, Jonathan Wood and James Harvey have played leading roles.

Lord Palumbo, Chairman, Serpentine Gallery Board of Trustees, and Chairman of the Jury of the Pritzker Architecture Prize, remains a key advisor for the Serpentine's Architectural Programme. We are indebted to him for his unwavering support, as well as to the Board of Trustees. We are privileged to have a group of Project Advisors for this year's Pavilion: we extend many thanks to Colin Buttery, Director of Parks, Royal Parks Agency; Ray Brodie, Parks Superintendent, Royal Parks Agency; Paul Lewis, Head of Operations, Stanhope Plc; Westminster City Council Planning Office; Jenny Wilson, Westminster City Council (Licensing Authority); Hassan Lashkariani, Westminster City Council (Building Control); and London Fire and Emergency Planning Authority for their support.

A number of companies have provided invaluable assistance in the construction of the Pavilion and with sponsorship help-in-kind. Some have supported our Pavilions in previous years and others are new to the project. Our sincere thanks are extended to all those listed below:

Ted Featonby and Mick Mead at Stage One for the skilled fabrication and construction of the Pavilion.

John Self at Elliott Thomas Group for providing site security both for the construction phase and while the Pavilion is open to public.

Richard Steer and Anthony Fowler at Gleeds for their management and construction consultancy.

Steve Jones at Laing O'Rourke for his expertise in construction materials and plant services.

Luca Virgilio and Kerstin Remy at Baglioni Hotel for their assistance with accommodation.

Banco do Brasil for their invaluable contribution, and in particular, our thanks are extended to Paulo Guimaraes, General Manager.

Barnaby Collins and James Penfold at DP9 for providing essential assistance with all aspects of the Serpentine Gallery Pavilion planning application.

Christopher Longmire at EC Harris for his construction, design and management skills.

Rupert des Forges at Knight Frank who guided the sale of the Pavilion.

Gareth Hardware at The Landscape Group for his continued assistance with external landscaping.

John Gaffney and Jon Fox at Site Engineering Surveys (SES) for undertaking land surveying and setting out the site.

Felix Rodel and Y. Didem Karakapici at Swiss International Air Lines for providing travel for the team.

We are also indebted to the Exhibition Circle for the 2012 Pavilion, who share our passion for the work of this remarkable design team. They include Lisson Gallery; Galleria Continua; Lillian and Jon Lovelace; Christophe W. Mao; Oliver Prenn; André Stockamp and Christopher Tsai; Galerie Urs Meile and White Rabbit Gallery.

The Independent is our media partner for the 2012 Pavilion and we are grateful to Simon Kelner, David Lister and Petra Luckman for working closely with us on this important project.

The Serpentine Gallery is proud to be a partner with Google Art Project. This collaboration is an opportunity to virtually experience all of the Pavilions from 2000 to 2012.

This year's Pavilion is part of the London 2012 Festival, a twelve-week UK-wide celebration featuring internationally-renowned artists, from Midsummer's Day on 21 June to the final day of the Paralympic Games on 9 September 2012. We have been delighted to work with Ruth Mackenzie, Director of the Cultural Olympiad, and Jenny Waldman, Creative Producer of London 2012.

The Serpentine Gallery acknowledges the Arts Council England for their ongoing support of the Serpentine Gallery Programmes.

We would also like to extend our thanks to the City of Westminster for all they have done to assist the Gallery.

We are indebted to Pro Helvetia and in particular, Pius Knüsel, Marianne Burki and Jelena Delic.

The Pavilion could not have been realised without the important contribution made by the Council of the Serpentine Gallery, and we are grateful to them for their continuing support of the Serpentine.

We are pleased to publish this catalogue as part of our ongoing series in collaboration with Koenig Books London. We acknowledge Franz König for his role in developing the series and express our gratitude to him and his team. We also extend our thanks to the inimitable Irma Boom and her office for the design of this publication. We are delighted to include an essay by Joseph Rykwert and we thank him for his insightful contribution. This publication features photography by Iwan Baan and Luke Hayes and we acknowledge their commitment to this project. We would also like to thank Melissa Larner for her editorial skills and Rebecca Catt for transcribing the interview with the architects.

This project has benefited from the skill and enthusiasm of the entire team at the Serpentine Gallery. Julie Burnell, Head of Projects, has once again led the Pavilion project and we remain indebted to her for the commitment and energy she has invested in realising the scheme. We would also like to thank Sophie O'Brien, Senior Exhibition Curator, who has been this year's Pavilion Project Organiser, supported by Claire Feeley, Assistant Curator. The *Park Nights* programme has been organised by Nicola Lees, Senior Public Programmes Curator, with the support of Lucia Pietroiusti, Assistant Curator, Public Programmes. Sarah Robinson, Head of Fundraising; Stephen Rider, Head of Finance; Katherine Holmgren, Head of Corporate Development; Rose Dempsey, Head of Communications and Tom Coupe, Head of Press, have also played essential roles in the realisation of the Pavilion and we are thankful to them for their hard work and dedication.

To the many individuals listed here, and to those not named who have also played a role in this important project, we remain immensely grateful.

Julia Peyton-Jones
Director, Serpentine Gallery and Co-Director, Exhibitions and Programmes

Hans Ulrich Obrist
Co-Director, Exhibitions and Programmes and Director, International Projects

EXCAVATING THE FUTURE

JOSEPH RYKWERT

Twelve years may only add up to the briefest of histories, but history it is for all that. The eleven annual Pavilions that precede this twelfth (and current 'Olympic' one) to be built on the lawn in front of the Serpentine Gallery have all been very different from each other both in plan and structure, although they all occupied the same space and were designed in response to the same commission.

The one rule that bound the choice of designers for those first eleven Pavilions was that they should be by architects of recognised merit, even celebrities, who had not as yet built anything in England at the time of their invitation. Each one of them would provide a welcome element of novelty for the architectural community – and even more, perhaps, for the general public. This is sure to be equally true of the twelfth one, though the rule has been bent a little on this occasion. Herzog & de Meuron did build the Laban Dance Centre in Deptford (2003) and – more famously – transformed the interior of the Southwark Power Station into Tate Modern (2000), and their project for its huge extension is half-built.

Ai Weiwei, for his part, made an installation of sunflower seeds in the same Tate Modern (2010). But this will certainly be their first joint and independent building in the UK – even if it is to be only a temporary one.

Herzog & de Meuron's enthusiastic and long-term collaboration with Ai – who manages to fit into one lifetime the activities of conceptual artist, film-maker and designer, as well as those of a very prolific architect and political activist – sets them apart from so many of their contemporaries, who tend to be loath to work with someone outside the corporate world of construction. They are perhaps also unique among architects in citing the approach of two artists (both very different) as their models and inspiration: the fastidiously reductive geometries of the American Donald Judd, and the radical dramatisations of the German Joseph Beuys. Equally few recent artists of whatever complexion have shown themselves eager to get involved in an architectural project or have given much thought to the place their work might occupy in the life of a building.

Of course, the two practices share many themes. A recurring one seems to be a fascination with the quintessential house type with its double-pitched roof. Ai made it the subject of his *In Between* installation in Beijing in 2000, and descanted on it in his Neolithic pottery museum in Jinhua, Zhejiang province (2003), while Herzog & de Meuron have made it the prime element when composing their VitraHaus (2009), a contribution to the Vitra Campus at Weil-am-Rhein. Their greatest joint achievement so far has been the extravagantly publicised Beijing National Stadium – nicknamed the 'Bird's Nest' – in which the 2008 Olympics opened. However minuscule the Serpentine Pavilion may seem when compared to the stadium, it nevertheless presents an intricate conceptual challenge.

What the informed spectator can expect from this collaboration is an acute awareness of material quality and an equally sharp appreciation of the project both as a geometrical invention and a conceptual intrigue. The architects' joint long-term interest in ecological issues and their dependence on re-usable materials is also on display – hence no concrete is used, structural or otherwise, but steel, timber and cork.

The nature of both task and site seemed to impose a fresh approach: their predecessors had each offered unrelated exercises in exploratory construction; every one of the Pavilions was different, contrasting, even aberrant. The primary design decision reached by the 2012 collaborators would lead them to disentangle that haphazard overlay so as to turn their contribution into a built dialogue between the new episode and the other Pavilions that came before – what was left behind when one Pavilion after another was taken down. This is now only a memory in the form of shadowy and disconnected detritus stacked up beside the Serpentine as the material remains of past centuries might appear on some other, more venerable archaeological site.

Each one of these eleven previous Pavilions had been an abstract invention – a built capriccio. The designers of this twelfth one take up the challenge to transform all the apparently random overlays into an architectural narrative, much as an archaeologist can convey purpose and vitality latent in what – to a lay observer – might seem ramshackle, dusty, overgrown wreckage. Of course, even the most sober of archaeologists will sometimes not content themselves with a prosaic reading of ruins, but will help them more or less imaginatively to deliver an account of what they once were: Sir Arthur Evans, when chided for the freedom of his reconstruction of the palace at Knossos, responded (punning atrociously): 'Well if it's not Minoan, it's mine own.'

What the 2012 new reading has produced is a rather perplexing but insistent geometry; it may look complex, but it is in fact quite spare: the prime and binding move was to sink a circular 'dish' (the designers' term) into the site – the circle being the most uninflected of all shapes. That circular sinking is hollowed out of the designated ground to the east of the Serpentine Gallery, and plays abruptly against the shadowy but very varied representations that the footprintsof all those previous Pavilions on the same site registered, so that what is recorded of them can be scried against this sharp circular outline and the overlay of the different plans. They are interlocked with such urban cabling as inevitably runs under the lawn to determine the labyrinthine moulding of the surface over and through which the visitors will now thread their way. This makes for slight, though occasionally abrupt, level-changes, which play against the circular outline as it slopes gently down from the south-east. The unstable and much-worked ground inevitably requires careful treatment, and it is therefore stabilised with timber decking over geotextile, while the sharper inclines are supported with wooden crib walls; the access and the paths around the site are also of timber decking.

The aleatory and therefore inescapably awry character of the surface is integrated, harmonised by a unified finish – a natural, compacted (and therefore somewhat darker than the raw material) cork. That surfacing transforms the 'dish' into a soft and welcoming underbelly, and its character is extended to the movable stools, all made of the same friendly material. They are designed so that they can be configured into different groups within the maze of the floor for both formal and informal occasions.

From the cork-lined dish – or rather thrust through it on screw piles – rise eleven straight supports, each one of them differently shaped, their number referring to the previous Pavilions, their shapes on plan suggested by the fitting into the interstices made by random encounters with the accidents in the site-plan. The twelfth support, representing the current Pavilion, is oblique.

A shallow, water-filled tray of 'invisibly' bolted steel sheet is supported on the columns; the segmental plan shape turns it into an almost full circle. That roofing disc is also displaced north-westward from the sunk and fully circular dish, so that the south-eastern crescent shape that results from the different diameters and the shift of centres is opened to the sky to invite day (and sunlight) but also rain into the covered space. It makes the structure into a steel – almost a high-tech – dolmen, with the difference that the steel upper deck does not act like a thick stone slab, but as a skin-deep, mirror-surface to reflect the surroundings; yet its archaic character is emphasised by the close and shallow space in the 'dish' – there are only 2.73 metres between its lowest level and the underside of the water-filled canopy.

That circle of the steel tray is crossed by a line that is drawn parallel to the edge of the Gallery, so that it only cuts a fraction of the slightly smaller of the two circles; it is, however, sufficient to allow a rare gesture of recognition to the usually neglected but charming existing Serpentine Gallery, built during the 1930s by a now largely forgotten architect, J.G. West. A straight wooden path leads from the Gallery to the Pavilion and removable steps allow performers access to the steel deck when it is drained for performances.

That hard, smooth steel and watery deck contrasts sharply with the knobbly surface of the dish sunk into the ground below, which is soft and welcoming, and the contrast between the two is an essential part of the project: a paradox that informs the dialogue that seems essential to the whole project.

A visionary and fabulous archaeology has offered the designers a formal device too complex – almost too wilful – ever to have been conceived without it. The Pavilion seems a miniature – because concentrated – reminder that our pavements and lawns often mantle and conceal the traces of our own past. Ai is perhaps most acutely aware of this, since China, more than any other country recently, has done away with a vast amount of its built past, and much of his work in China has been bound with celebrating and commemorating these rapidly vanishing remains – like the Hutong houses that are echoed and applauded in his courtyard homes and installations.

Ai and Herzog & de Meuron have therefore offered London a unique architectural narrative, and moreover, one brilliantly condensed. A narrative in building is not a fashionable concept – in fact, the death of the 'great narratives' has been something of a commonplace theme of recent criticism. The architects have pushed the boundaries of their discipline to investigate the possibilities of much smaller – even, as at the Serpentine, almost miniature – responses to such circumstances. The Beijing 'Bird's Nest' Stadium offered a declaration that was unique and startling because of its giant scale. At the Serpentine they have shown that architectural narrative can be equally intricate and fascinating in miniature.

THINKING AND BECOMING

HERZOG & DE MEURON + AI WEIWEI

Every year since 2000, a different architect has been responsible for creating the Serpentine Gallery's Summer Pavilion for Kensington Gardens. So many Pavilions in so many different shapes and out of so many different materials have been conceived and built that we tried instinctively to sidestep the unavoidable problem of creating another object, a concrete shape. Our path to an alternative solution involves digging down some five feet into the soil of the park until we reach the groundwater. There we dig a waterhole, a kind of well, to collect all of the London rain that falls in the area of the Pavilion. In that way we incorporate an otherwise invisible aspect of reality in the park – the water under the ground – into our Pavilion.

As we dig down into the earth to reach the groundwater, we encounter a diversity of constructed realities such as telephone cables, remains of former foundations or backfills. Like a team of archaeologists, we identify these physical fragments as the remains of the eleven Pavilions built between 2000 and 2011. Their shapes vary: circular, long and narrow, dot-shaped and also large hollows that have been created. These remnants testify to the existence of the former Pavilions and their more or less invasive interventions into the natural environment of the park.

All of these traces of former Pavilions will now be revealed and reconstructed. The former foundations and footprints form a jumble of convoluted lines, like a sewing pattern. A distinctive landscape emerges that is unlike anything we could have invented; its form and shape is actually a serendipitous gift. The plastic reality of this landscape is astonishing and it is also the perfect place to sit, stand, lie down or just look and be awed. In other words, it is the ideal environment for continuing to do what visitors have been doing in the Serpentine Gallery Pavilions over the past eleven years. The Pavilion's interior is clad in cork – a natural material with great haptic and olfactory qualities and the versatility to be carved, cut, shaped and formed.

On the foundations of each single Pavilion, we extrude a new structure (supports, walls, slices) as load-bearing elements for the roof of our Pavilion – eleven supports all told, plus our own column, which we place at will, like a wild card. The roof resembles that of an archaeological site. It floats a few feet above the grass of the park, so that everyone visiting can see the water on its surface reflecting the infinitely varied, atmospheric skies of London. For special events, the water can be drained off the roof as from a bathtub, from whence it flows back into the waterhole, the deepest point in the Pavilion landscape. The dry roof can then be used as a dance floor or simply as a platform suspended above the park.

Herzog & de Meuron + Ai Weiwei
May 2012

Working together by video conference, we discussed our aim to create a Pavilion that was casual in attitude, not too heavy, to fit the temporary nature of the brief.

We wanted a place that was open to all, for people to come as part of their park experience and have a meditative moment; a place with a simple beauty, like feeling a light breeze.

Instinctively, we tried to sidestep the unavoidable problem of creating an object, a concrete shape. Could we try to achieve something that was 'non object'?

One of our initial thoughts towards realising a non-visible project was to reveal the groundwater and collect rainwater.

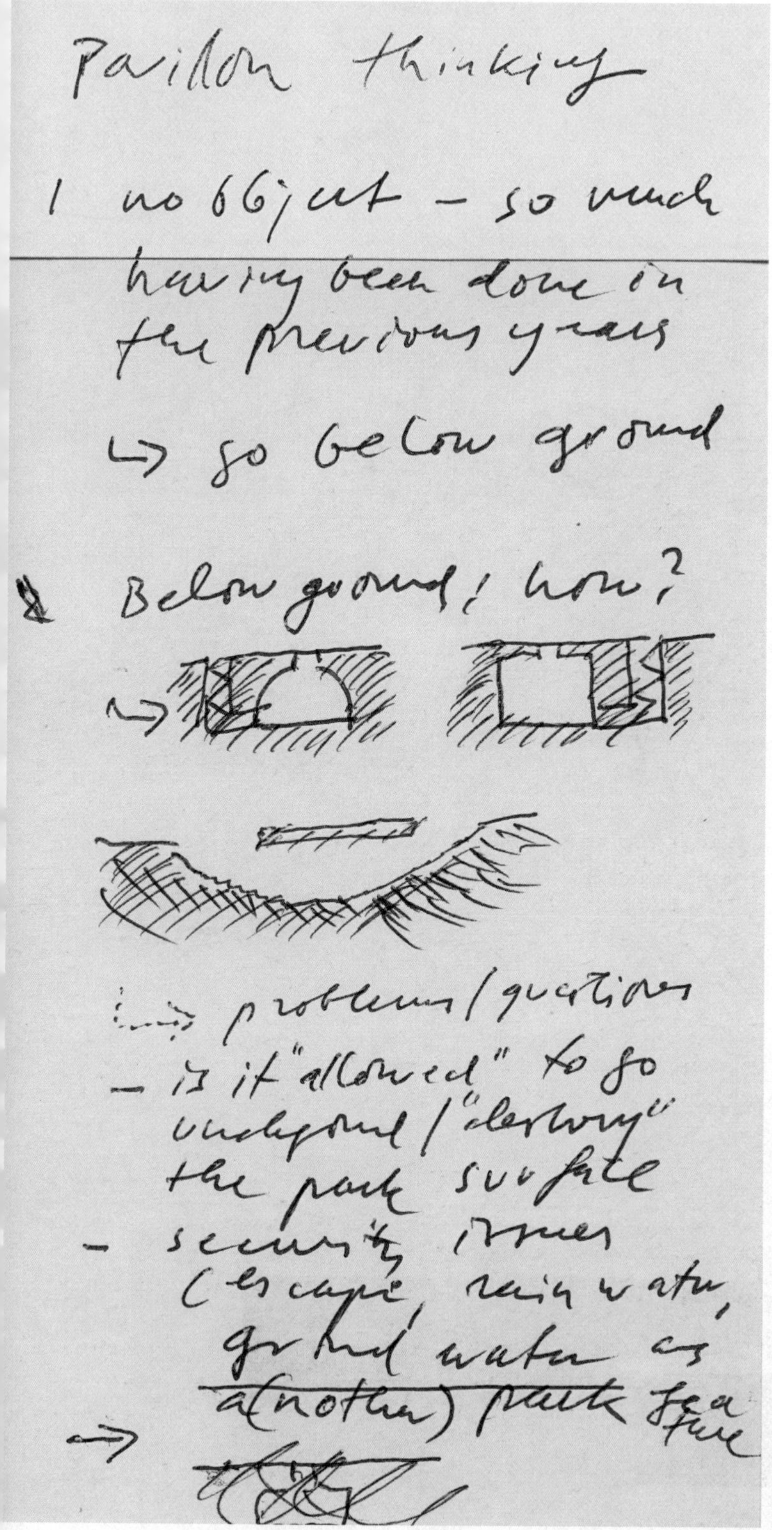

Pavilion thinking

1 no object – so much having been done in the previous years

↳ go below ground

Below ground; how?

→ problems / questions
– is it "allowed" to go underground / "destroy" the park surface
– security issues (escape, rain water, ground water as a(nother) park feature

→

This led to thinking about excavating a deeper area, and even going below ground.

We thought the Pavilion could be an underground space with mirror walls that would bring together people and water, sun and rain, and the changing conditions of the London sky.

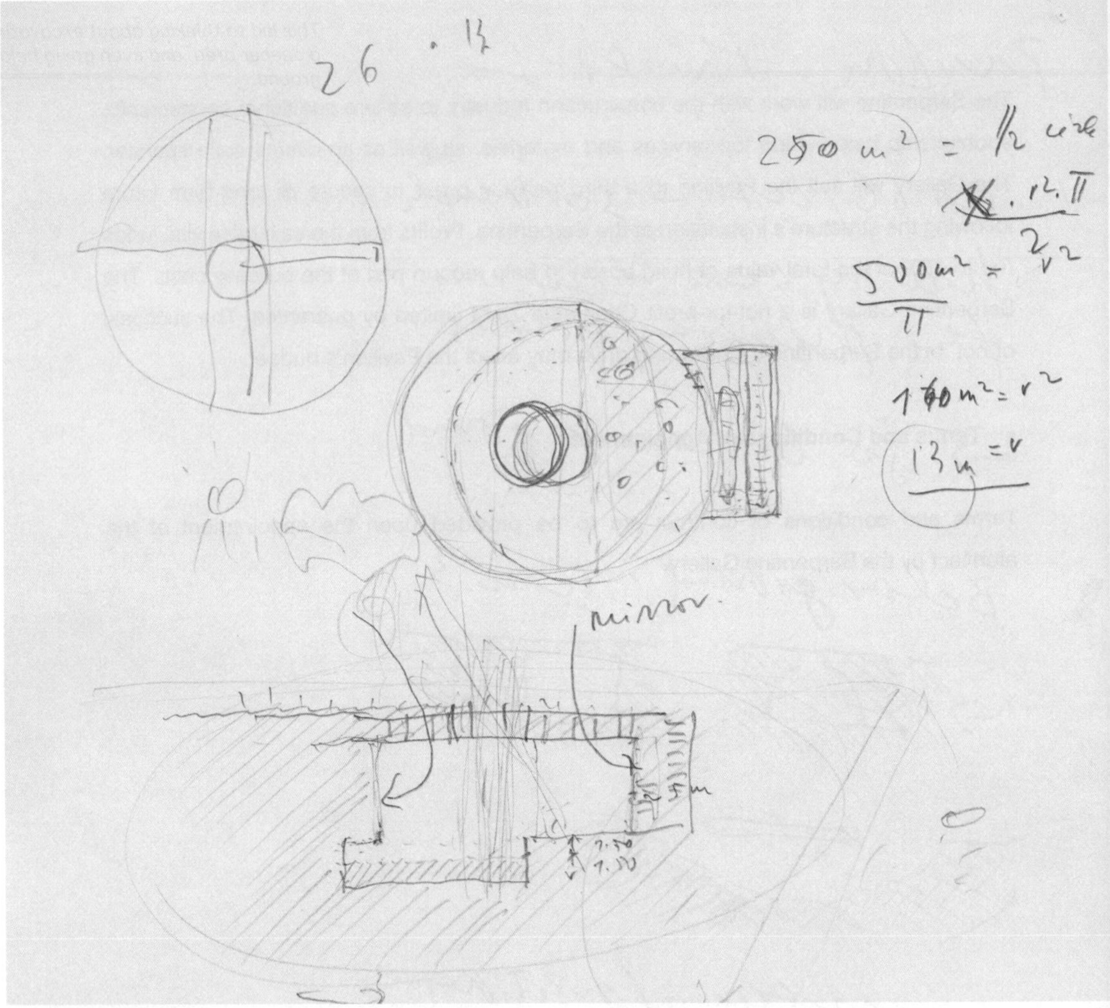

However, we soon understood that a completely underground Pavilion without any physical expression above ground wasn't possible.

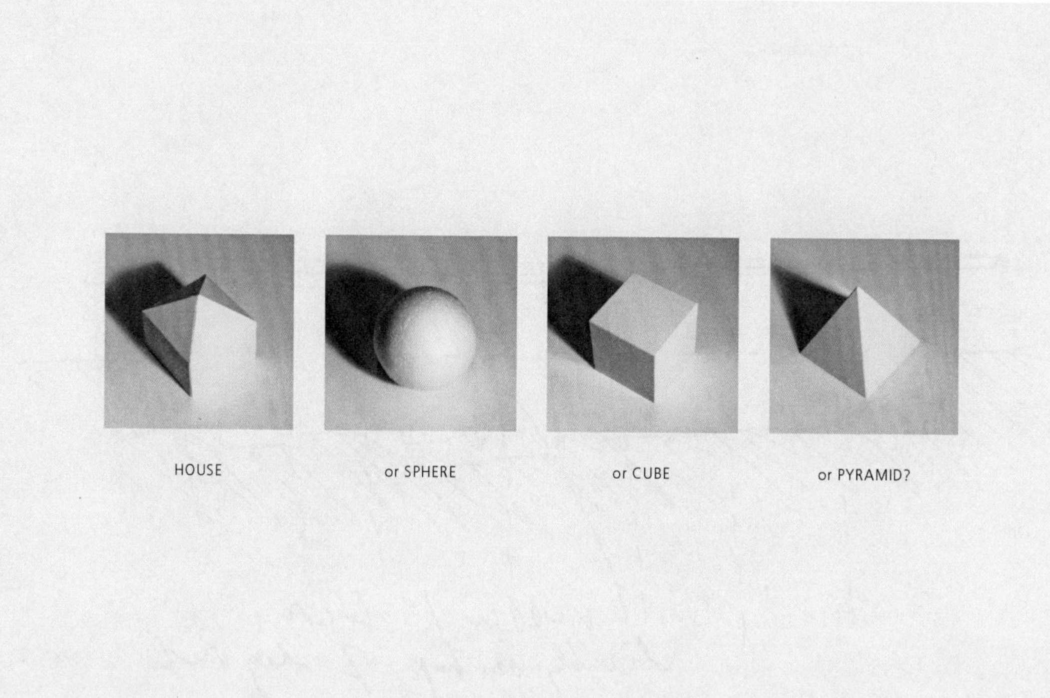

We looked at an above ground Pavilion that, while visible, would be as independent as possible from formal vocabularies, expressions and tastes. We found that this authorless quality could be best expressed in familiar volumes, pure geometries and platonic forms.

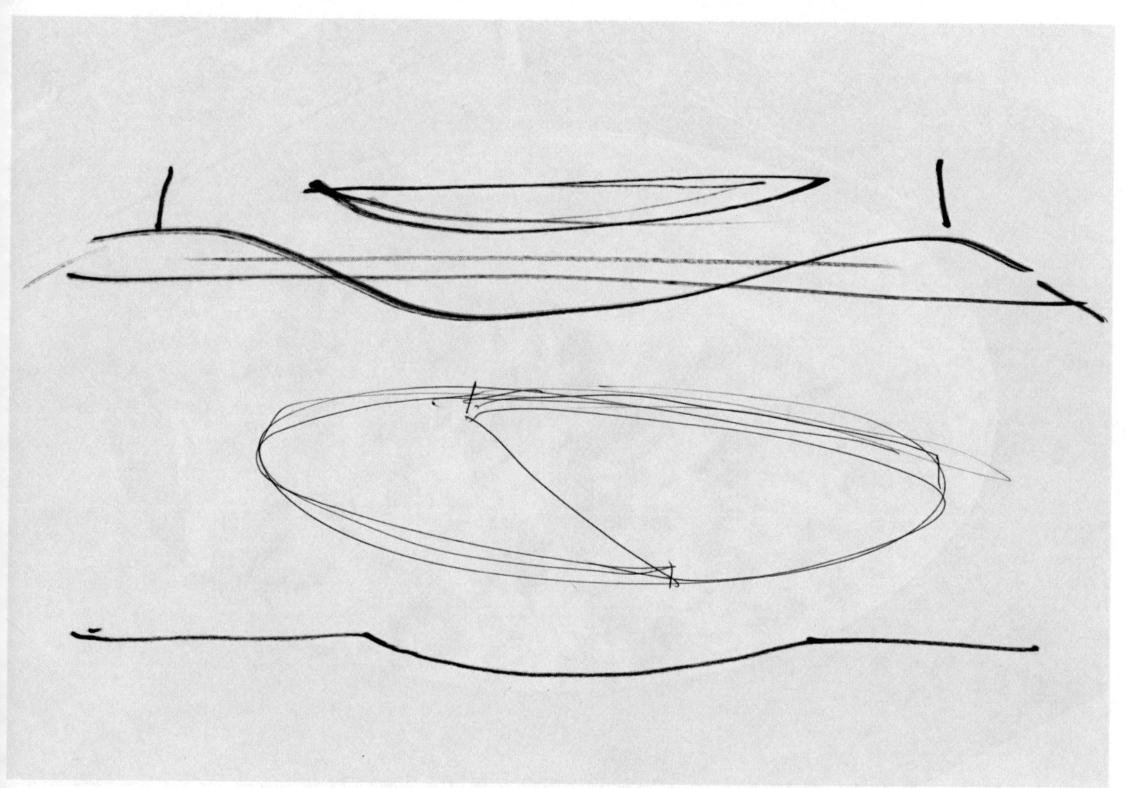

Yet we were still attracted to the sunken form. We found that we could dig down, but were advised not to go below 1.5 metres, or several feet, because of the groundwater.

By going below the surface, we wanted to offer a surprise, another landscape, another park. We thought that this discovered landscape could be a kind of amphitheatre or a dish, not too deep.

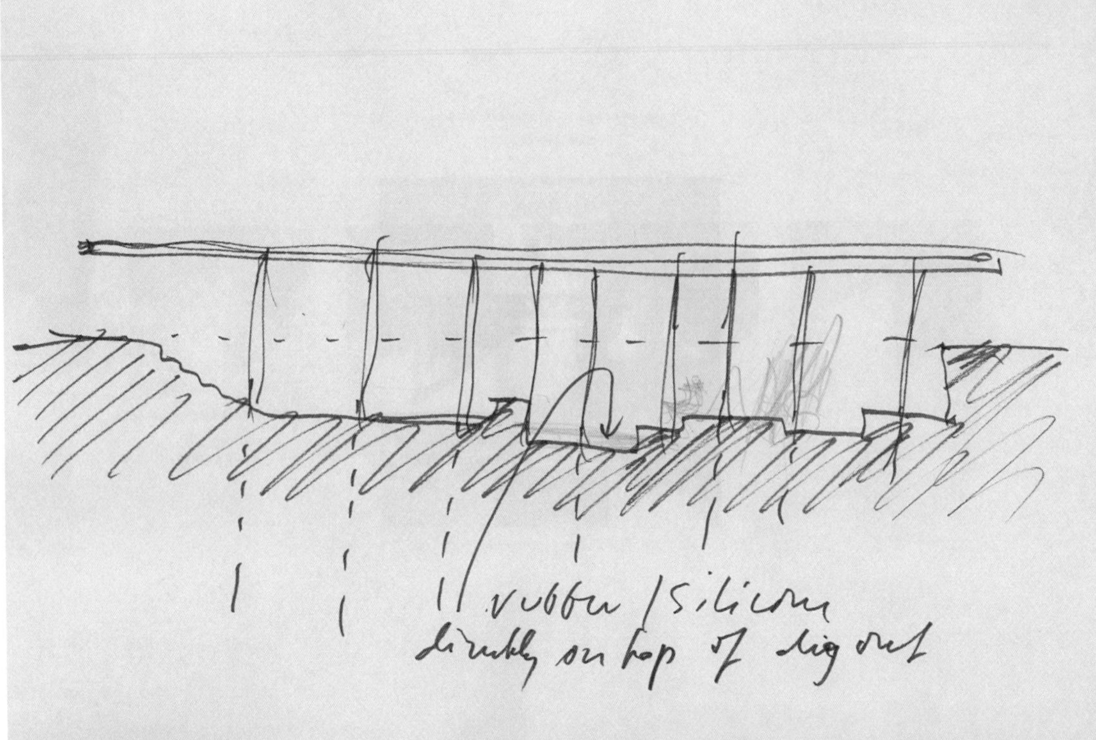

The ground could shift, going up a little and down a little, to encourage people to move around it. And it could be used for lectures, performances, dinners and relaxation.

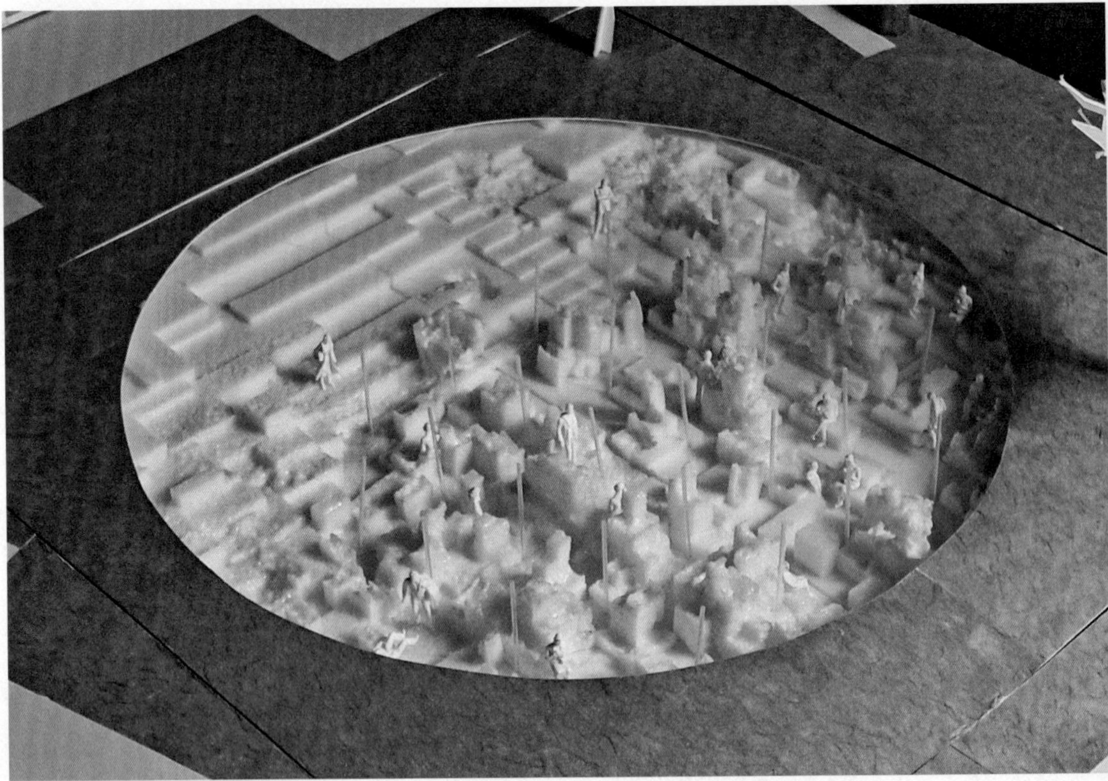

We tested ways to produce an abstraction of the landscape with a playful quality...

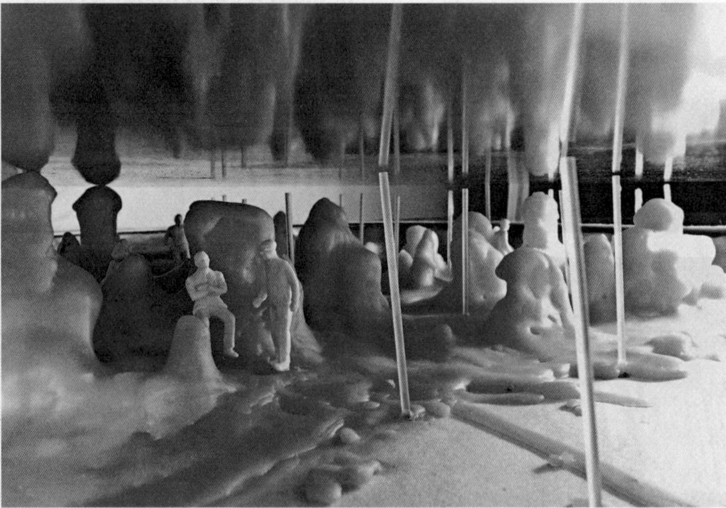

...maybe like melting candy or the bubbles of boiling water, covered in rubber or silicon.

We thought about translucent materials, like a cloud, but eventually agreed that an opaque, almost monolithic approach would work better since it provides an architectural presence that you have to experience.

Not forgetting our earlier concepts for an underground space, we thought about a sheltering roof – something light, ephemeral and simple.

We looked at a compact disc, interested in it as an approachable form that could provide a simple roof – flat, circular and thin – with a hole that could provide natural light and water drainage.

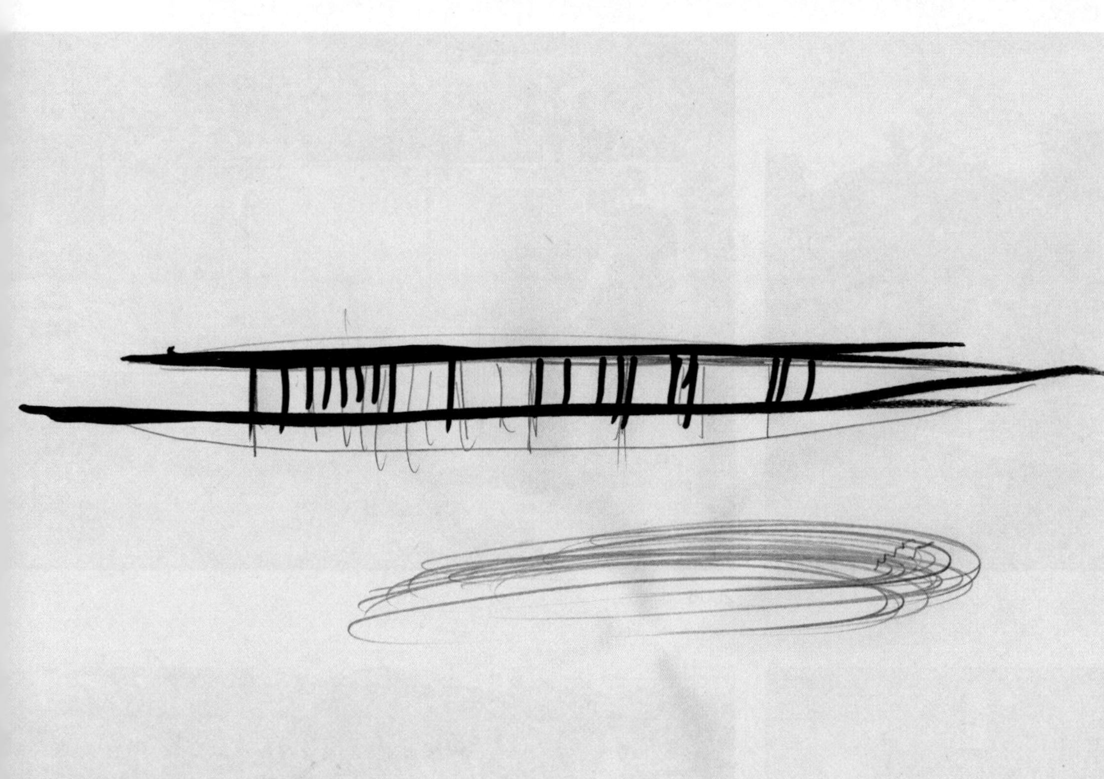

It could even be a very low ceiling that people can touch. In contrast to the abstract landscape, it could be a perfect circle.

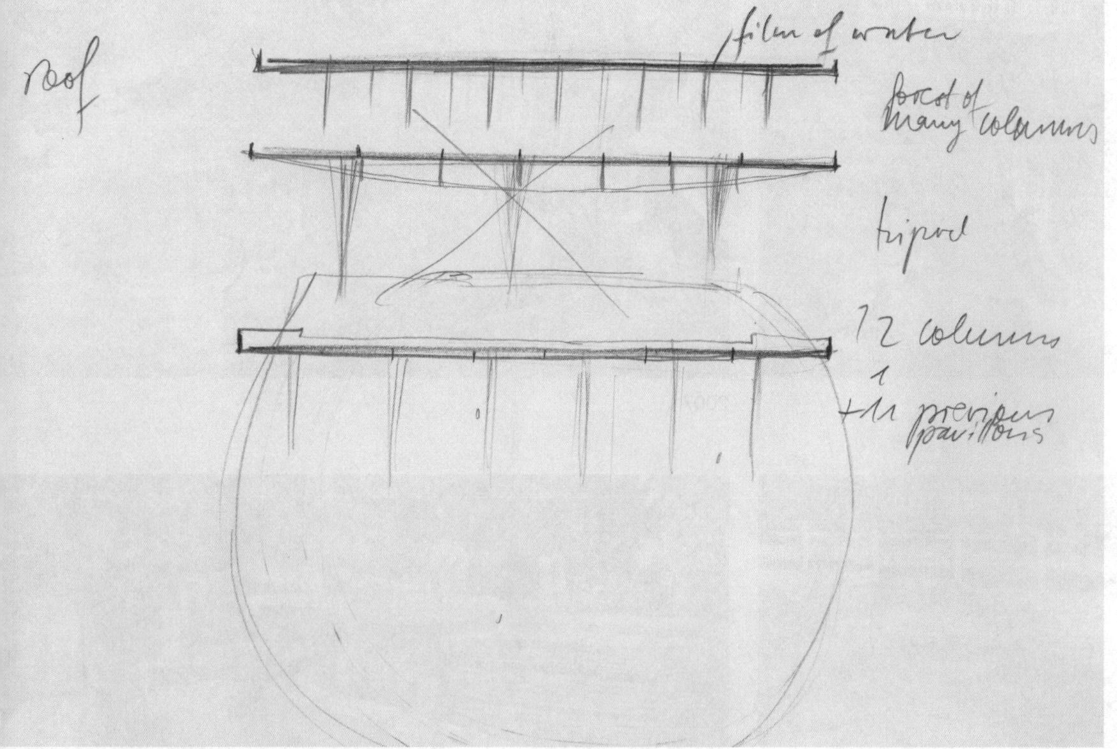

We thought about how this roof could be supported. It could rest on a very heavy base – three hills of excavated earth and rock which could form part of the landscape itself – or on something very light, like thin columns or inflated cushions of air.

2002

2003

2005

2006

2007

2008

2009

When we looked at the ground conditions of previous Pavilions, we were surprised to find a history of extensive foundations in the seemingly innocent gardens.

2010

2011

2008 2009 2010 2011

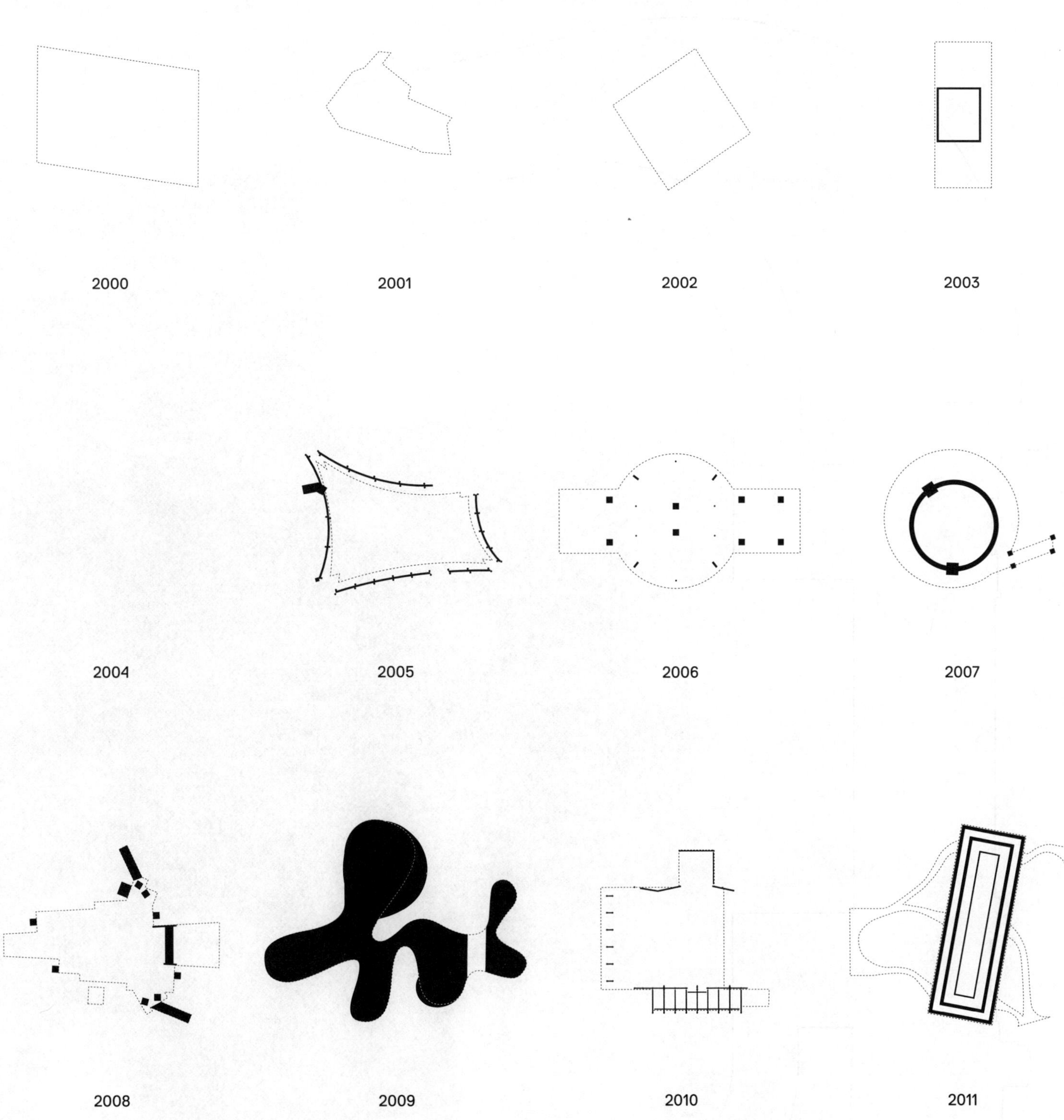

By studying the history of this small patch of grass, and outlining the footprints and foundations of previous Pavilions, we could reveal their ghosts. The Pavilions don't remain physically, but their traces do, like a readymade, or like buried treasure.

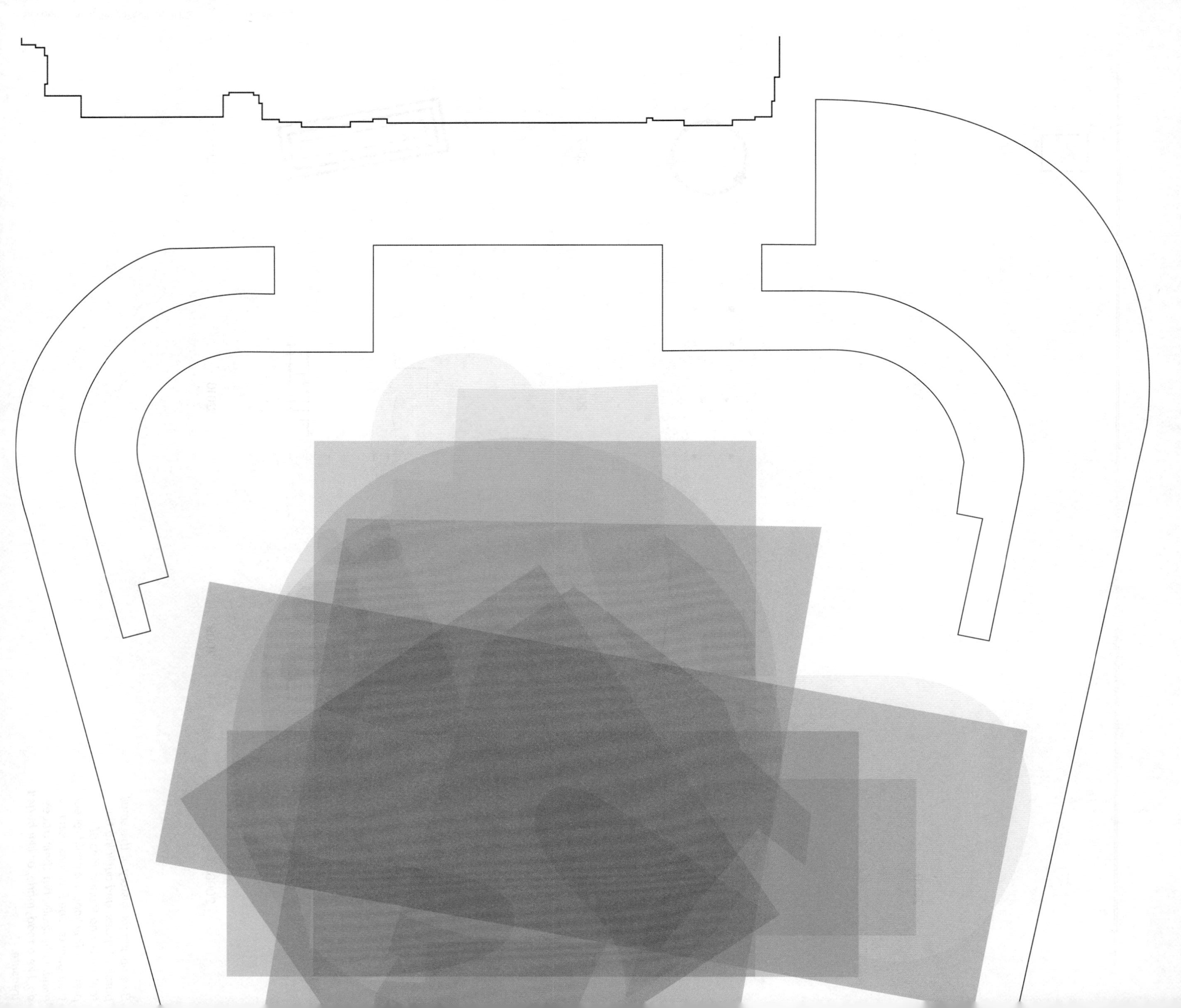

We overlaid the above ground footprints of previous Pavilions.

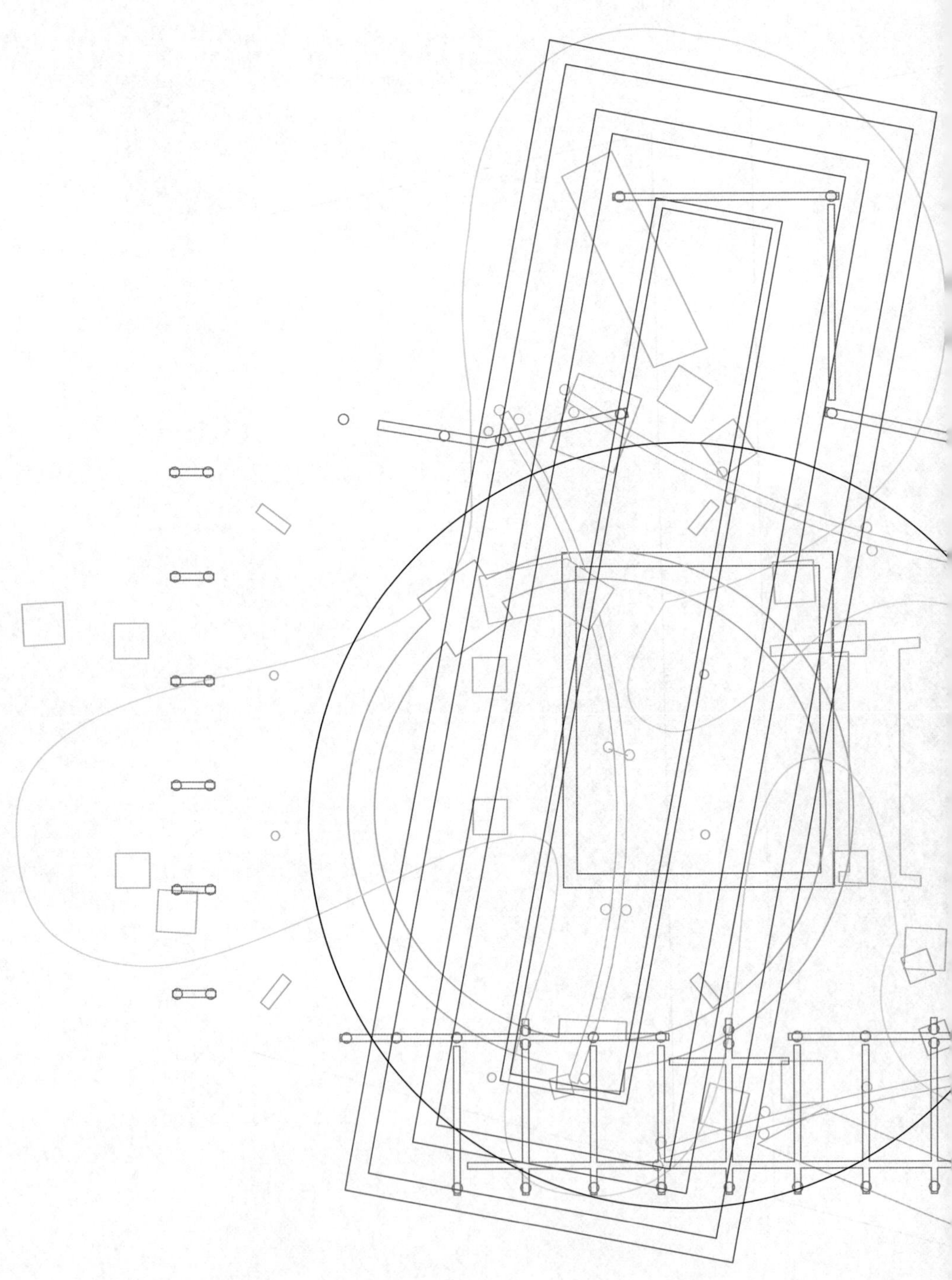

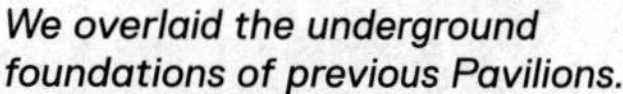

We overlaid the underground foundations of previous Pavilions.

2011 (Peter Zumthor)
2010 (Jean Nouvel)
2009 (Kazuyo Sejima + Ryue Nishizawa / SANAA)
2008 (Frank Gehry)
2007 (Olafur Eliasson and Kjetil Thorsen)
2006 (Rem Koolhaas and Cecil Balmond, with Arup)
2005 (Álvaro Siza and Eduardo Souto de Moura with Cecil Balmond – Arup)
2003 (Oscar Niemeyer)
2002 (Toyo Ito and Cecil Balmond, with Arup)
2001 (Daniel Libeskind with Arup)
2000 (Zaha Hadid)

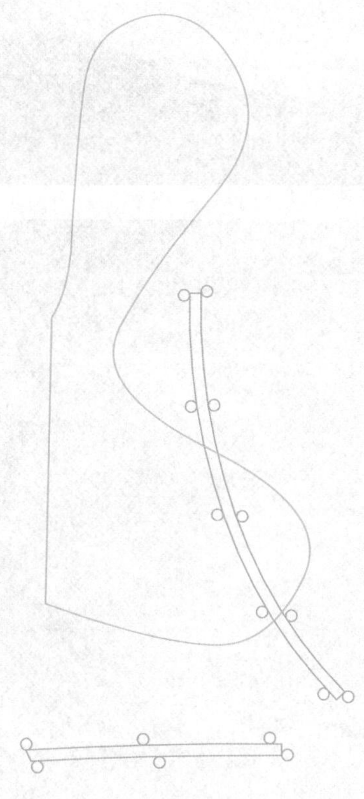

A distinctive landscape emerged in response to the pattern of former Pavilions. The overlapping shapes and density of footprints define the surface topography, while the previous foundations are reconstructed for seating and extruded to become roof supports.

A simple, plainly artificial metal roof is placed asymmetrically, to allow an amphitheatre-like feel on one side, and the possibility to access the rooftop on the other.

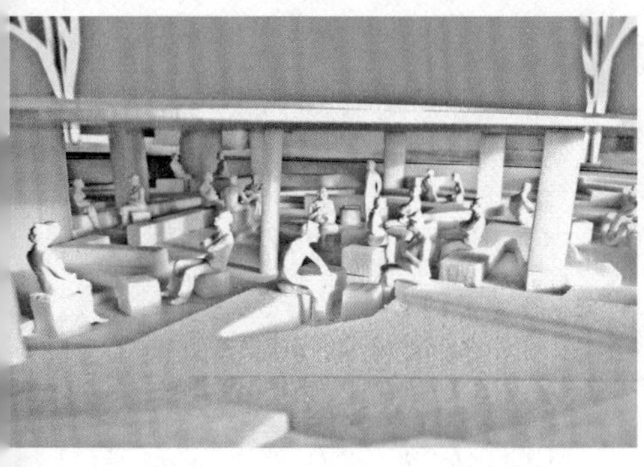

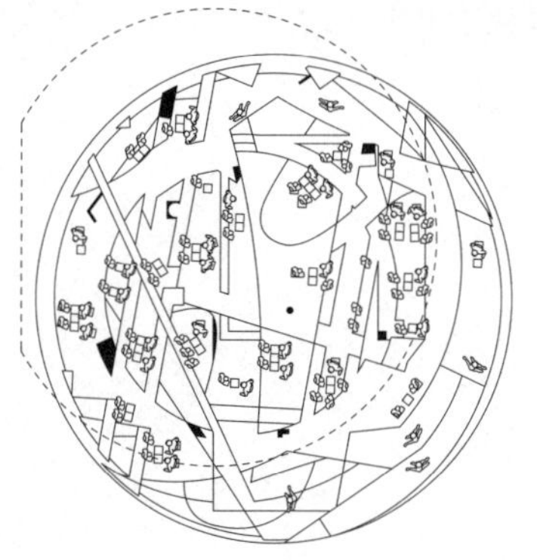

Café

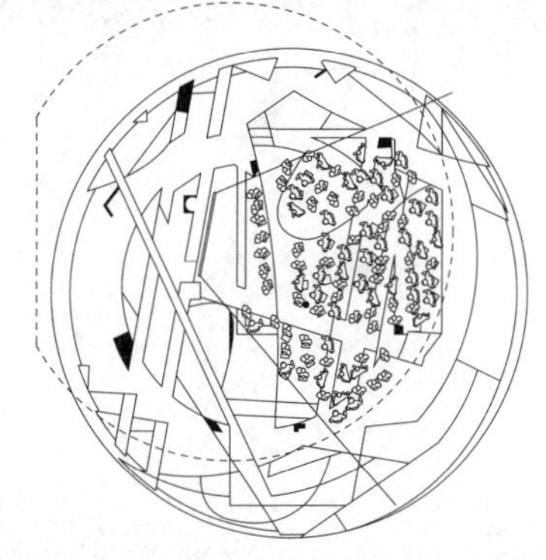

Screening

Lecture

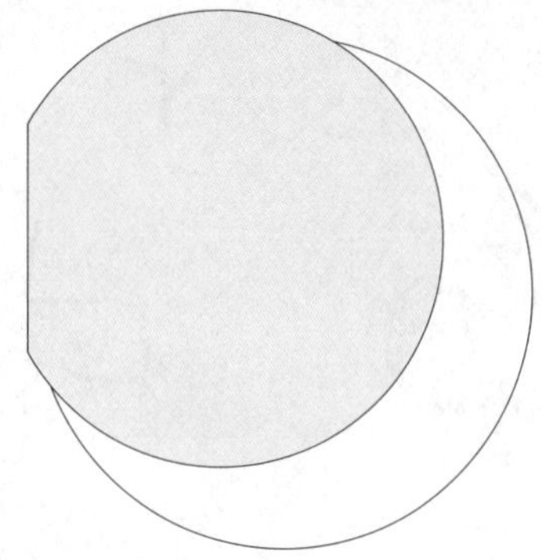

Water

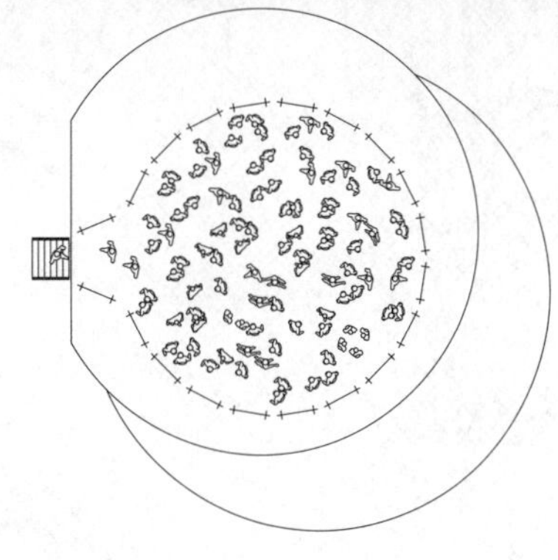

Event

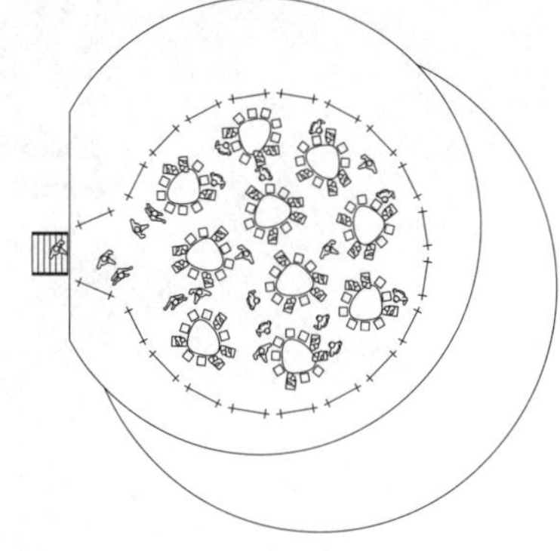

Dinner

^ *The Pavilion is dynamic in terms of its uses. The landscape offers surfaces that can respond flexibly to various planned events such as lectures and dinners, and unplanned activities such as stretching and reclining.*

^^ *The roof is also responsive and flexible, acting like a mirror of water during the day with the possibility to become an event space at night.*

The roof is supported by twelve columns: one to represent each of the previous Pavilions and a new one for 2012. The columns are located close to their ideal structural points in a polar distribution.

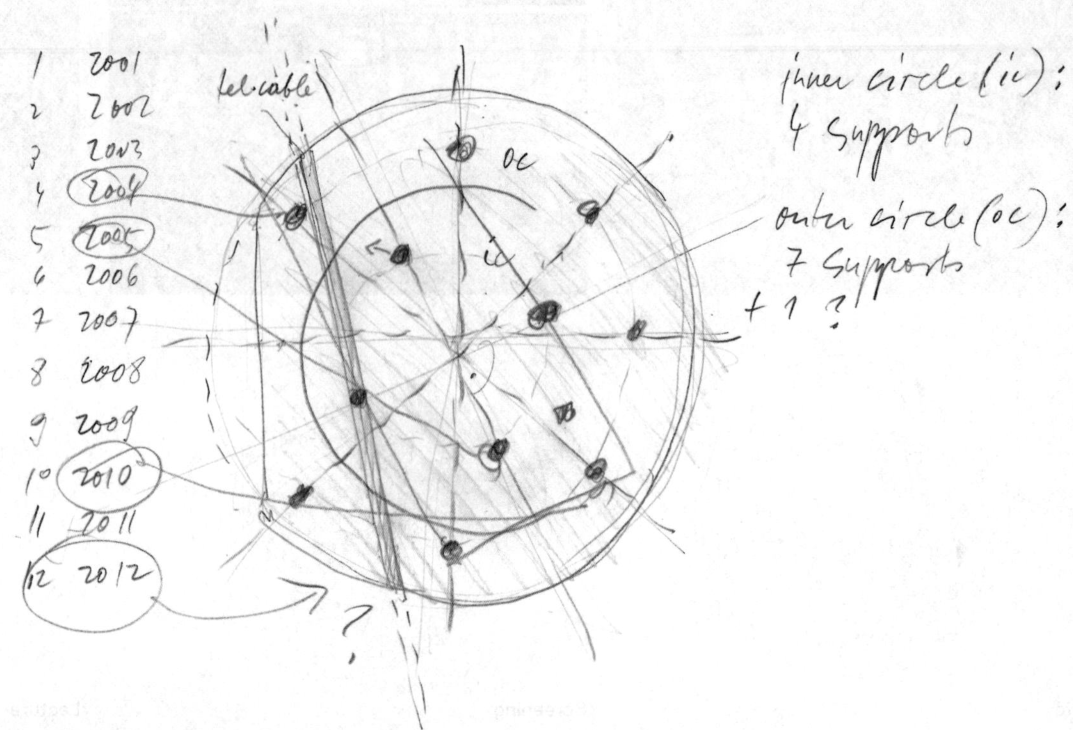

As in the landscape, the shapes of the columns are generated by the intersecting outlines of the former built elements.

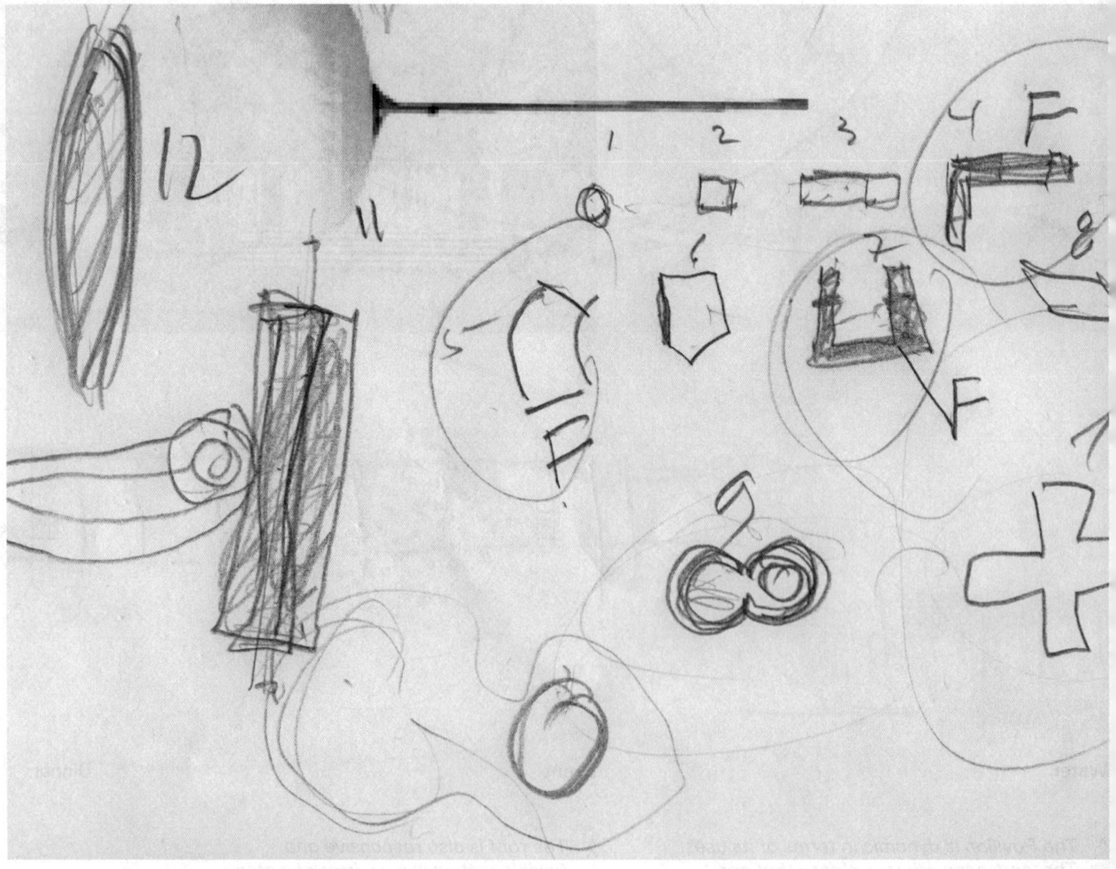

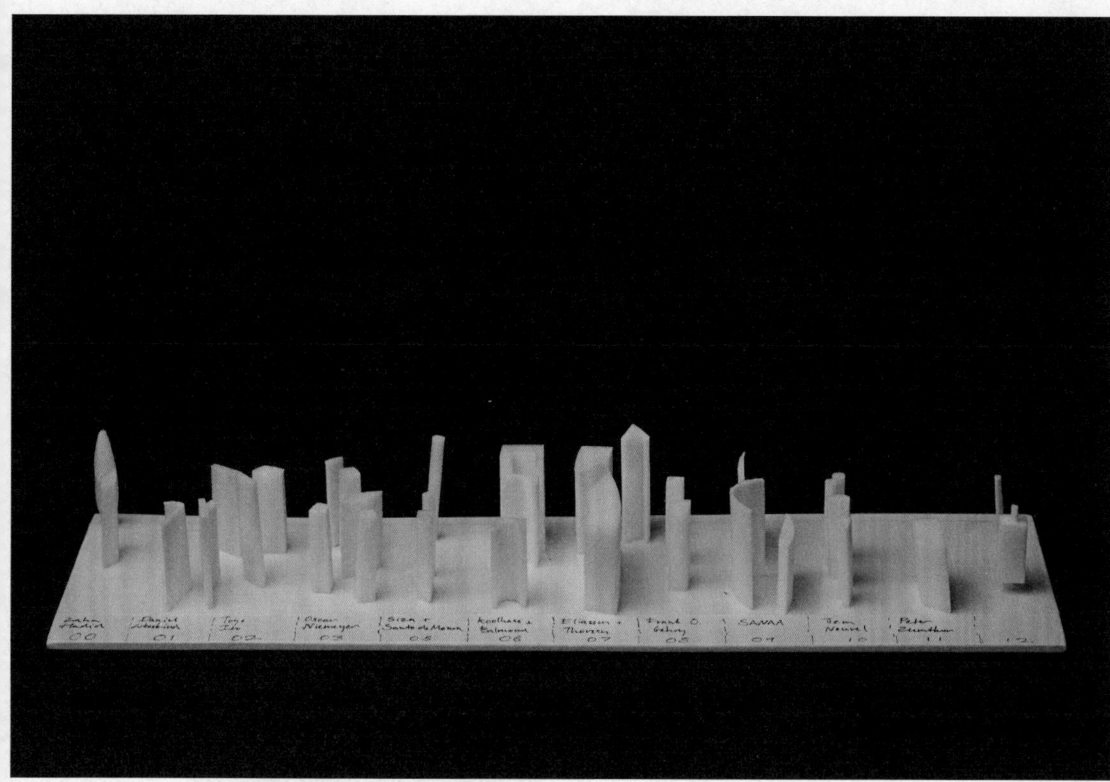

The different logics and conditions of previous Pavilions come together and generate a complexity that we could not have invented on our own...

... and the possibility to develop a collection of abstract forms in a language that would not normally be used.

2009
2011

2003
2010
2011

2001
2002

2005
2007

2001
2002

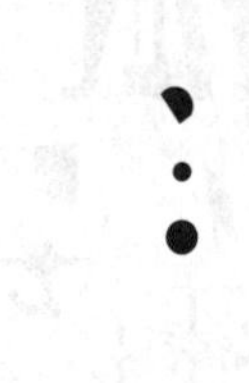

2005
2006
2010

2007

2010
2011

2000

2006
2008

2003
2006
2008

2005
2010

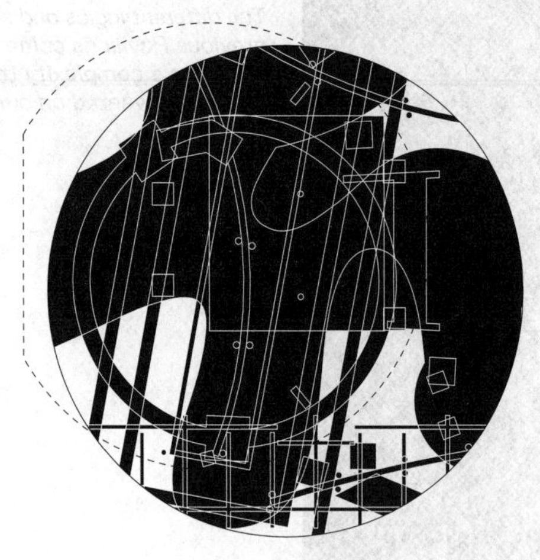

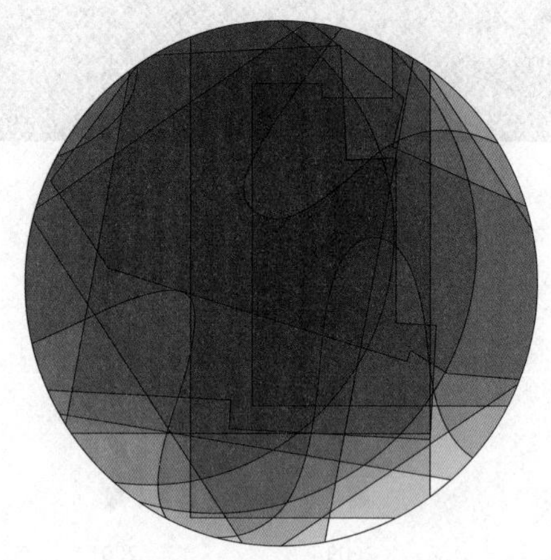

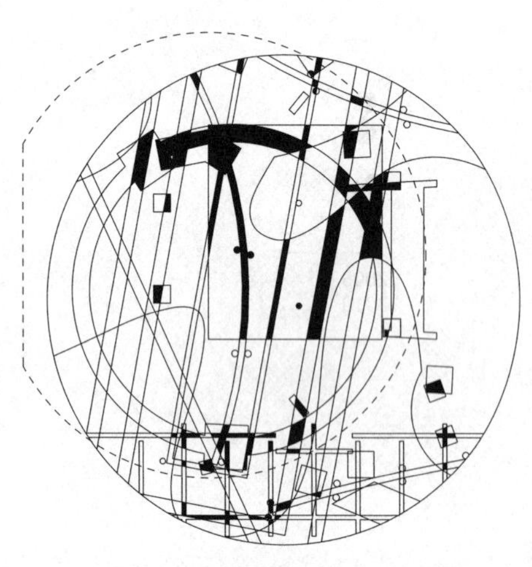

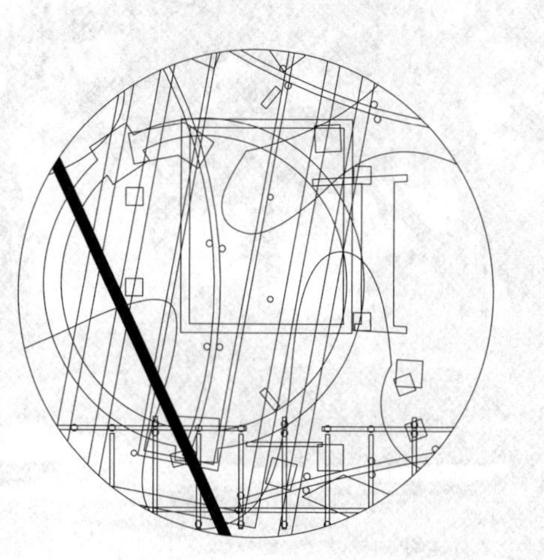

Instead of creating a new fantasy, we wanted to allow the existing complexity to generate something different and playful, but in a straightforward way.

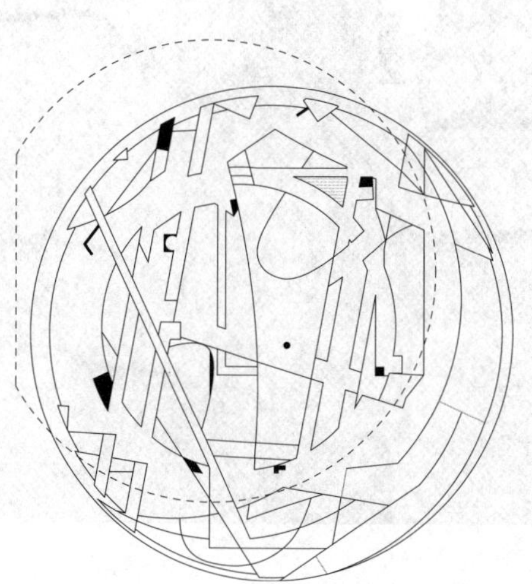

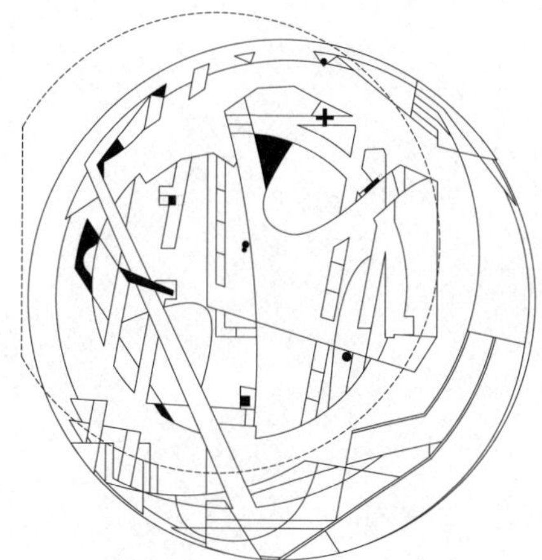

From the beginning we wanted to work with cork, a naturally versatile material with great haptic, olfactory and acoustic qualities. We explored its many conditions from harvested raw sheets of bark to processed composite blocks. The solid cork blocks absorb the colour and smell of smoke during the molding and heating process, where natural resins are activated as binders.

Sloping the sides of the underground dig reduces the amount of soil excavated and avoids the use of heavy retaining walls. A timber decking and geotextile system is placed directly on the earth, without the need for conventional concrete foundations. The cork cladding is cut, shaped and sanded into many forms on-site.

Sheltering roof.

Traces of all previous Pavilions.

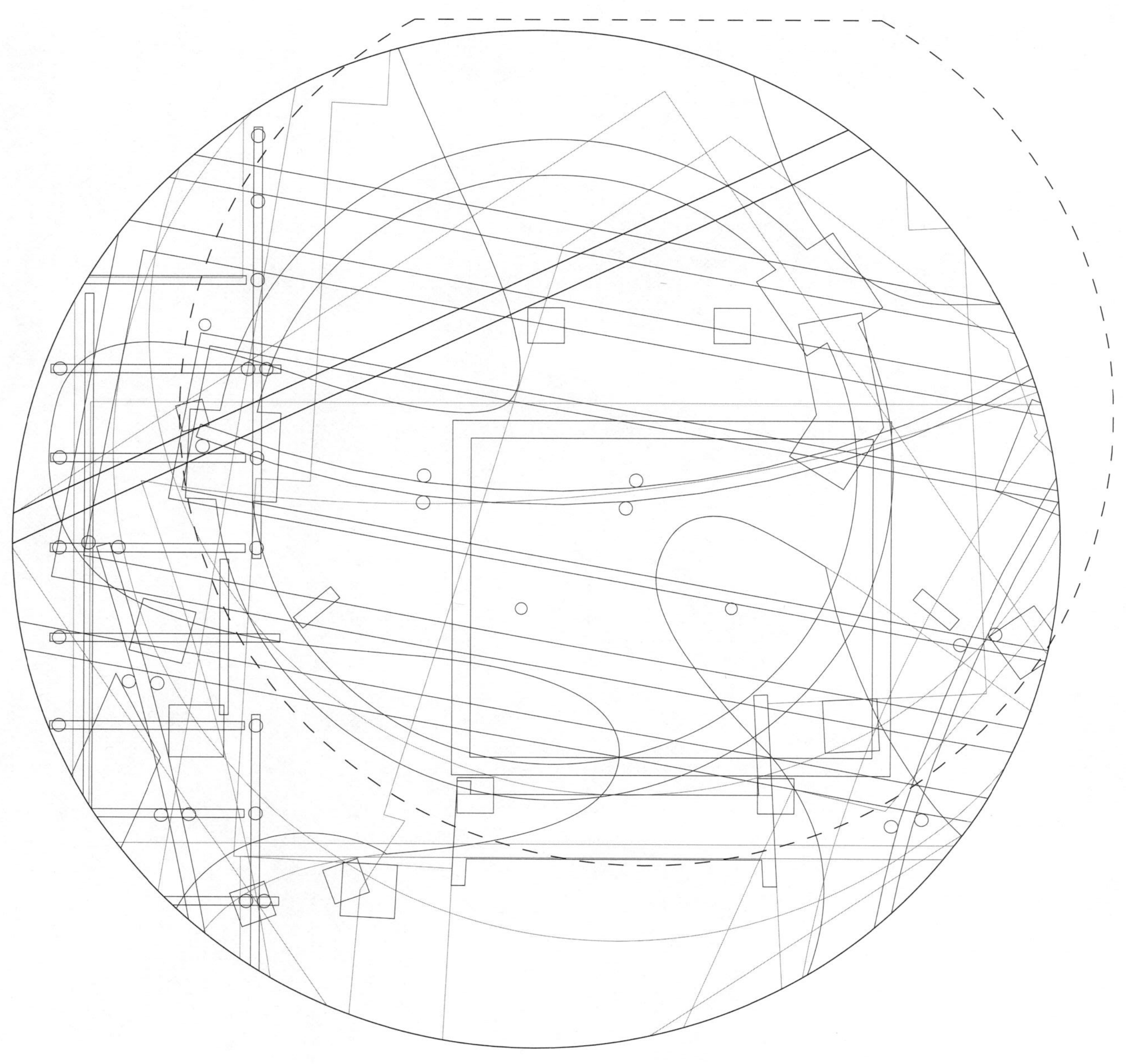

Overlay of previous footprints.

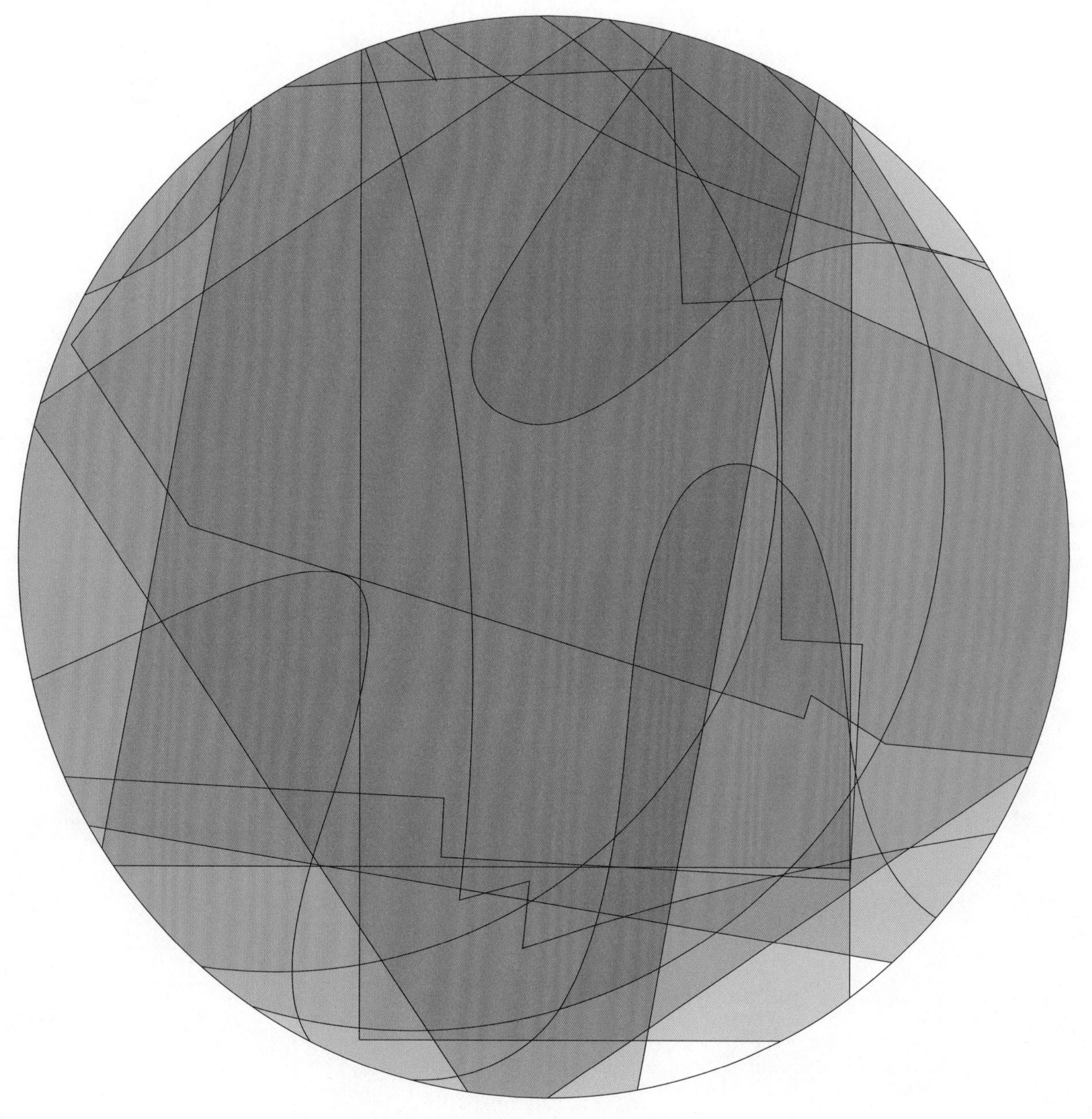

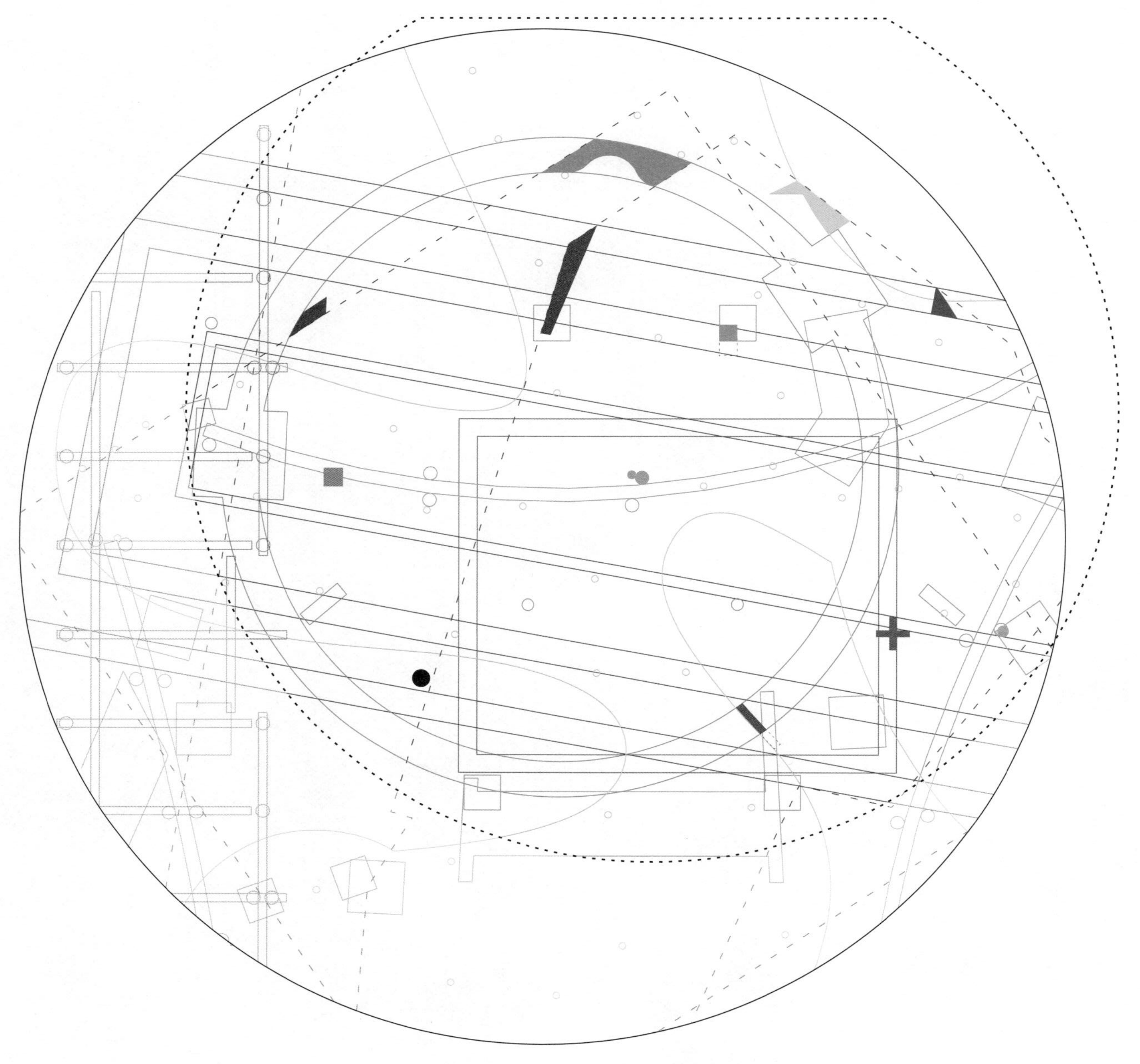

Twelve columns.

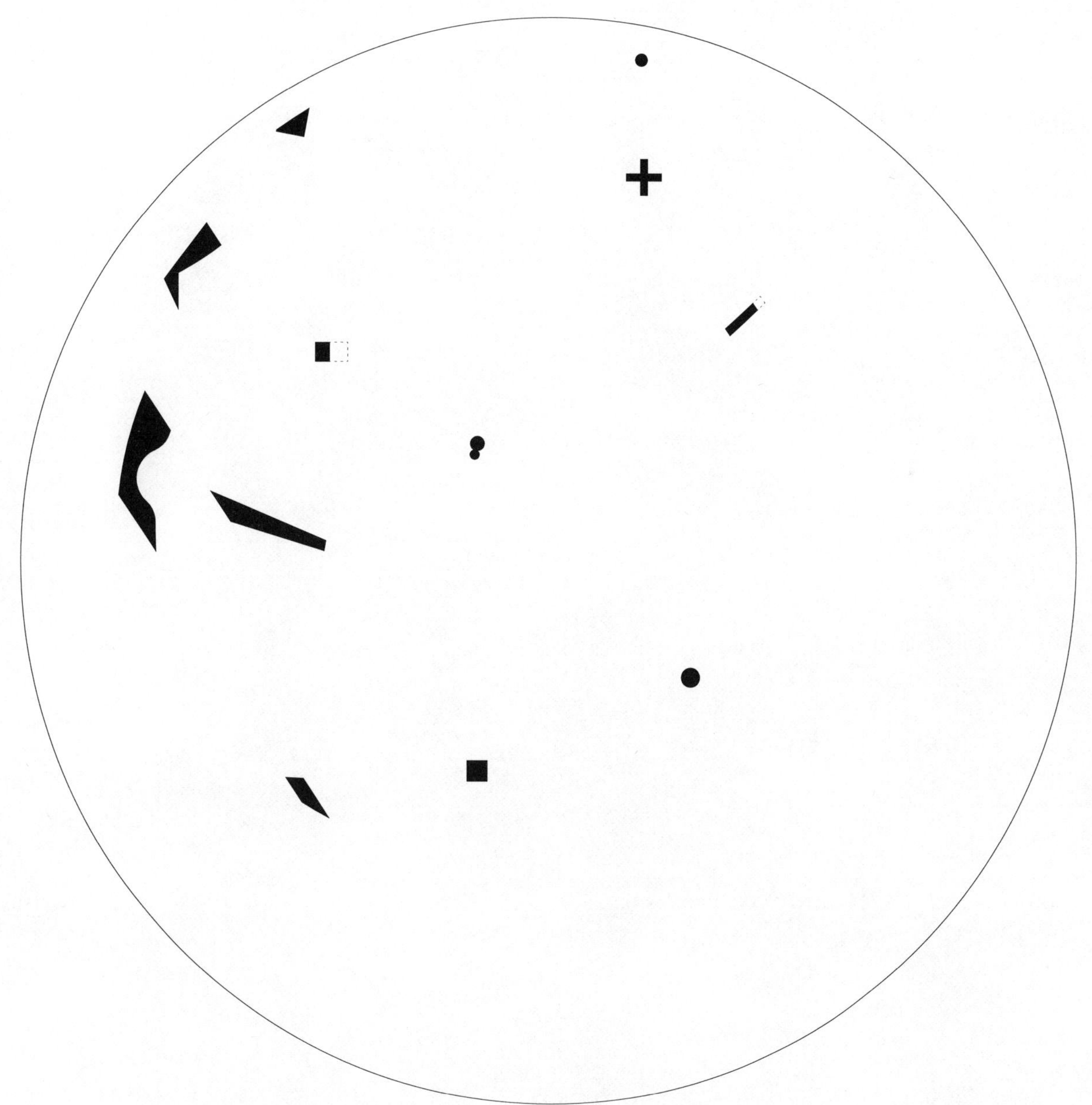

Extruded landscape.

Cork landscape.

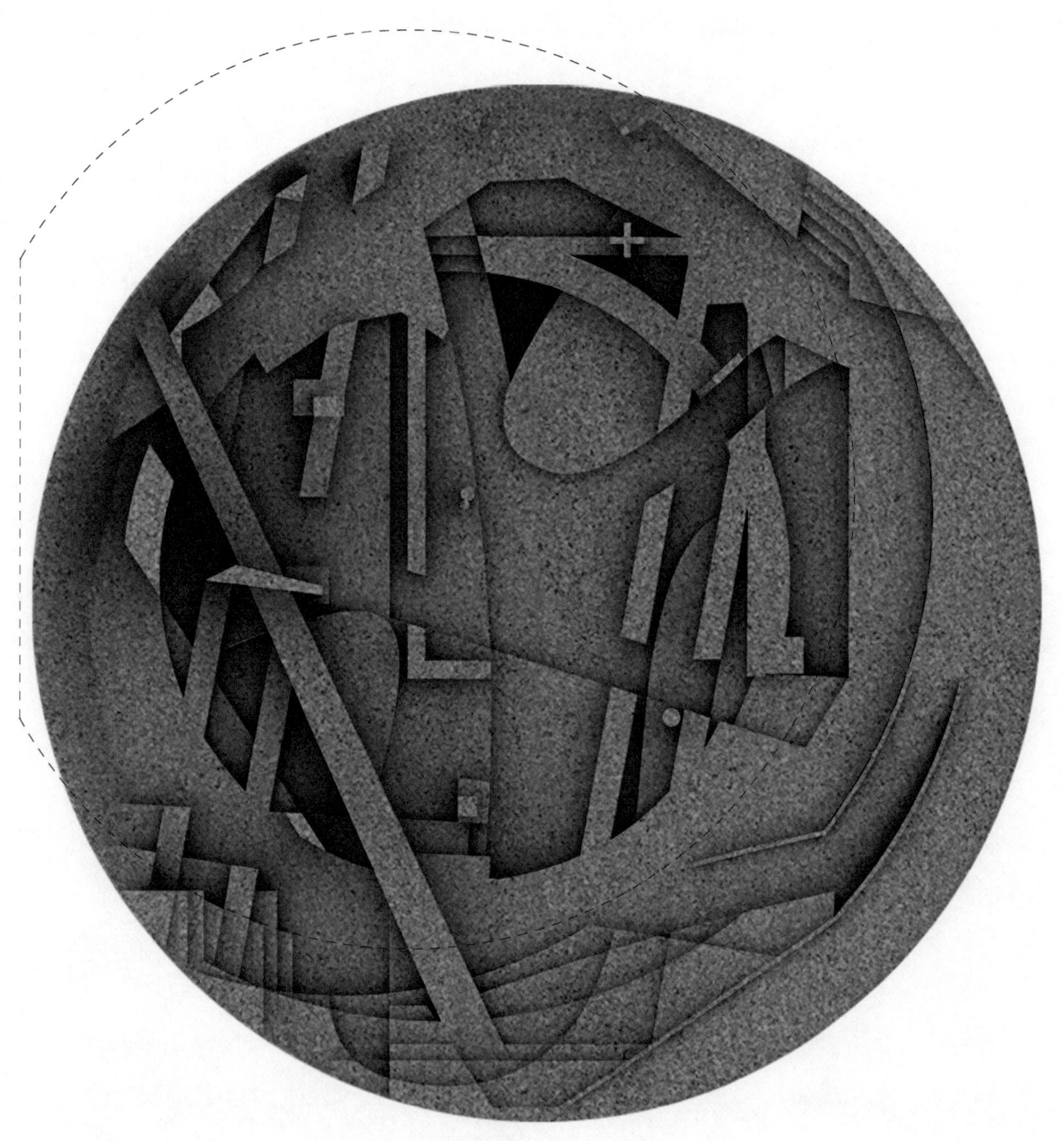

Water mirror.

A CONVERSATION JACQUES HERZOG, PIERRE DE MEURON AND AI WEIWEI

WITH JULIA PEYTON-JONES AND HANS ULRICH OBRIST

JPJ The closeness of the friendship and working collaboration between the three of you is very clear to see. Hans Ulrich and I also work together closely in tandem, and people always want to know who does what. Does the 'who does what?' apply to your work on the Serpentine Pavilion?

JH It's been more than ten years since we first met Weiwei in Basel, and we all travelled together to China due to his friendship and generosity and interest in bringing something new to his country. The Serpentine Pavilion is our first project together in the West. It was a very natural feeling to work on it together. It was as if we'd never stopped collaborating and that, I think, is very important. The project has nothing forced about it, nothing artificial and nothing where you could say 'This is Weiwei and this is Pierre and Jacques.' It all comes out of our common experience of what we've seen and what interests us and what we've learnt from all these different trips. That's how I, at least, have experienced it.

AWW My experience of working with Jacques and Pierre is that we never think separately. It's like three soldiers in the war – and that's a good feeling: we have a constant understanding of each others' practice. We never have any arguments during our collaborations. We always come together and create the support for the whole idea, making it possible. It's always a very enriching experience for us, very encouraging. There's no ego or any kind of need to assert one's identity because from the very beginning we said that we were working, the three of us together, on a new identity: we're working together to create a new style. So there's this connection that's very special. It's also difficult for us to see art and architecture as separate. For me they're quite inseparable. And that's why I have an interest in this kind of activity.

HUO The 'Bird's Nest' Beijing National Stadium [*commissioned for the 2008 Beijing Olympic and Paralympic Games*] is one of your great architectural collaborations. How was this idea born? Was there a moment when you had the epiphany or was it a gradual process that led to this masterpiece?

AWW The stadium was a moment of excitement because it was a utopic event, from an architectural point of view and from a political point of view. We all understood that we had to make something that was powerful and that would remain as a long-lasting monument. So we tried to do something that was very different from the previous understanding of stadiums, and we wanted to give it a strong signature. We came to an idea very quickly; we always get to the idea very quickly, because we all kind of agree.

JH The speed and the mystery of collaboration is key to our working together. Pierre and I have been collaborating since our childhood, so to us it felt natural to collaborate with an artist. We'd already done this with Thomas Ruff and with Rémy Zaugg. And so Weiwei was just a new element in our life – a very precious one, however! Ideas happen on a common ground and then it's not A + B + C, but a dynamic that's more complex. And the fundamental layout of a concept is indeed sometimes very fast. It's like the blinking of an eye – the feeling that someone loves what you're saying or that you love what the other person's saying and that encourages you to go deeper. It was the same with the Serpentine Pavilion.

JPJ What's so interesting about our site is that it now has an eleven-year history of Pavilions, and what you've chosen to do is to look back to the archaeology of past Pavilions and create a kind of fiction – it's a fiction based on fact, but nonetheless a fiction. This access to the old and the new is the pivotal element of this project. How did the idea of making reference to the past, the present and therefore also the future, come about?

AWW This idea about the archaeology of past Serpentine Pavilions comes down to the fact that architecture is a total effort, as a history and as a human structure. We tried to make something very essential, very visceral; we wanted to put ourselves in a position where we could have a conversation with other people's efforts and to make a very clean and understandable gesture out of this.

JPJ Did this approach to architecture as a total effort feed into your thoughts regarding the design of the Pavilion?

JH We all three of us shared the idea that we didn't want to make another object or another thing in Kensington Gardens, but that we wanted to literally build a foundation for something different, something new. And the interesting paradox is that this foundation for something new or different is exactly what has been done before. The Pavilion design is very important in our fundamental approach, which is a re-thinking of what a pavilion actually is, or what a stadium actually is. I think that's probably what keeps us going through all kinds of projects: what actually is this thing we have to build? There's so much architecture and so much art and so many things in the world that if you don't do this radical questioning then you end up in endless repetition.

PdM We came to a very quick agreement on what we didn't want to do. From the first moment, we knew, all three of us, that we didn't want to fall into the trap of doing another fancy object, because this has been done in previous years. So we had two possibilities: one was to use platonic forms, which are universal: a sphere, a pyramid or a cube. But this wasn't successful. But this is the benefit of working together as Jacques and myself work together as a pair: always having someone to correct you or give you another answer or another direction to the process. This avoids getting stuck, or maybe having ideas or elements that are too personal. And now it was just a case of enlarging this two-way relationship into a triangular relationship with Weiwei. So having abandoned the platonic volumes, we then became interested in finding geometries or forms of something that was already there but was, on the other hand, no longer there, since it had been demolished. So things are virtually there but no longer physically there. We found out that there were some traces underground that were not visible. So we were interested in discovering and analysing what had been done in previous years, and in revealing those traces and using them as generating forces for our design. After having made this choice to work with those traces, it was a matter of deciding which traces to select for our final design. We'd already spoken about not doing an object, not even doing an object proposal. That was one thing and the other thing was this fantastic site in the park. And when the first ideas started coming, we were more interested in doing something hidden, something that wasn't visible, something underground. Of course, this wasn't going to be easy, but it was a very important start for the project – to have it below ground. Then it emerged that it wasn't very realistic because of the groundwater and other problems. But this idea to have it buried continued to carry the whole process of exchange of ideas. And then we decided to have it half-buried and to cover it with a roof to protect the space.

HUO Cork has the versatility to be shaped and formed and it is often used in making architectural models. Why did you use cork to line the interior of the structure?

PdM Architecture is a discipline that speaks to people through all their senses. It isn't only visual but tactile and acoustic, and we were interested in having different elements in the Pavilion. The water on top is ephemeral, reflecting the sky and the light from above, and all the surroundings. The steel structure to carry that water and to protect the people under the Pavilion is heavy. So where the people touch and move around within the volumes of the space, they need to have this softer material, something warm, so that they can sit on something that's warm and soft with a very tactile quality.

HUO This idea of an archaeology of the past connects with the topic of memory. We live in a digital age where information grows exponentially, but that doesn't necessarily produce more memory. We could even say that sometimes amnesia goes hand in hand with this information explosion. I remember having a conversation with Weiwei in Beijing about memory, in relation to this obliteration of moments in the past. And there is a wonderful text [*which appeared on Ai Weiwei's blog*] where you talked about bringing your mother's house back to its previous condition. Now, for your Pavilion, memory plays a big role: it's the memory of the previous Pavilions and the memory of the site. Could you tell us what memory means for both of your practices in general? And beyond that, what memory means in relation to your Pavilion?

AWW In the very beginning we wanted to look at the psychology of the Serpentine Pavilions that have repeatedly been taken down, which we saw as being like an act of total architecture, or a stage – a stage that was repeatedly dealing with architecture. The past structures might have a very different energy and a very different background, but still they shared the same kind of understanding, and we wanted to use our understanding of it to make a Pavilion that could conclude this kind of total effort, as well as showing the tension between the very different styles and the effort to re-announce it. So we saw the past as a psychological condition, like drawing many layers on one piece of paper. And normally that isn't an architectural quality. But we felt the need to create something very different.

JH As both Pierre and Weiwei have said, because we're a team, not only the two of us, but also with Weiwei, our architecture becomes something that's free from a personal style: a style-less conception, or a concept-based approach. I think this is typical of Weiwei's working method as much as it is ours. We've always tried to replace style with concept. So memory is just an excuse. Is it also a real interest? I think it is in the sense that how a building touches the ground is a fundamental question in architecture, something that goes back to the very first human structures. Also in classical architecture, the foundation is a key element. And to free the object from the earth is a key issue in modernism and Constructivism – all those flying objects also deal with the same issue. When you look into Weiwei's work, you see that he's been obsessed with digging into the ground in some of his earlier projects...

AWW Of course, this desire to make something underground – it's like any child: they want to dig up the sand or play with mud; it is an absolutely essential human activity.

JH ...and we can find it in our own history already in the early work of the 1970s and the 80s. One of the first projects that we did that became known was a proposal for a fountain in the Market Square in Basel [*1979–87*] where we dug into the ground and revealed a hidden river. This was key for understanding how the city was originally built and how life was generated around that river, all of which had been forgotten. Revealing the medieval river completely transformed the perception of that part of the contemporary city.

HUO The historian Eric Hobsbawm famously said: 'I belong to a profession whose business it is to protest against forgetting – which also knows that memory is complex and sometimes dangerous'. Very often the future is built on the fragments of the past, so we need memories, but at the same time, we can't create work based only on the past because it can be suffocating. What is the relationship between remembering and forgetting in your work?

JH This could be a very interesting and fundamentally human question. Without memory, we cannot build a future, but too much memory is a burden. This is a very fruitful paradox.

AWW I think that we have to realise that we're a product of information and since human survival is very practical, the most reliable information is gained from history that has been collectively approved. At the same time, of course, as humans we have a problem because we're always trying to find another imaginative possibility, which is about trying to overcome the tension between living and dying – the idea that you're there and then you're not there. This is so simple; we're all fascinated by this and it's why we all have to see if we're any different. So every project, if it's a good project, has to have this kind of mysterious quality that makes us wonder. And if it's not a profound concern and becomes too superficial and too shallow, then we're simply talking about the past or tradition, which isn't interesting at all. We have to find a new possibility, a new way, a new definition in some kind of common ground.

JH This could be a very fruitful and productive question for the *Marathon* discussions in the Fall. [*Every year the Pavilion is host to the* Park Nights *programme, and in 2012 this culminates in the staging of the* Memory Marathon, *which draws its inspiration from the Pavilion.*] It would be interesting to involve people who can talk about this from a scientific point of view and not just art or literature. As you said in your question, it is a kind of paradox: it's very dangerous in some ways that we tend to forget things and make the same errors that we made in the past and if you look at human history it's tragic that the same patterns come up again and again. Nevertheless, history repeats many things, but not exactly the same way. With our Pavilion design, of course, we use the traces of all these quite wonderful objects that have been created in the past, each of them with much love and with much talent. And I think what will happen is that people will come to the Serpentine and many of them will have seen the Pavilion last year or three years ago or five years ago and they'll try to read the traces. They'll somehow reconstruct history or memory, trying to remember what they've seen here. So what I think is interesting is that it's a kind of virtual architecture becoming physical or perhaps even more: a physical architecture triggering memory. It wasn't our intention, but probably the concept will lead to the architecture that's absent, that doesn't exist anymore. It will help people to remember their own lives, which I think is a nice idea for architecture.

JPJ You're going to allow people to become time travellers, to retrace their lives and provide them with the context to do that in a completely democratic space: a structure without walls. Your Pavilion, in that sense, is one of the most democratic spaces that you could possibly come across, much more than the Serpentine Gallery itself, because there's no barrier to prevent people engaging with the structure. It is the ultimate act of generosity, like a present. And indeed, Richard Rogers described the Pavilion as the greatest gift that is given to London every year. How important to you was this idea of creating an accessible public forum?

AWW I think we're all very interested in public space and in the need to have some kind of public meeting space. We realise that we only have one page in the Serpentine Pavilion 'book' and then this page will be turned over by another effort. So this project will be inserted into the whole effort. When we talk about memory, it's about an understanding of the past and at the same time, of the fact that one day we're going to be the past. So I think that gives a very special understanding of this kind of architecture. And it not only stays in our minds, but it stays in the public mind. So that's why I think this project has a very special meaning beyond the architecture itself. This idea of public-ness and our understanding of what a public building is: it's not about personal tastes, it's about the memory or history that we have to recognise. It doesn't matter whether we like it or not; it's there and it's up to us to make it very public. This is a very interesting approach that could give a new definition to public sculpture.

PdM The projects that we've been developing together with Weiwei and also all the ones that we've been working on in our office are mostly public and some of them are highly public. I don't think there are many buildings that could be more public than the 'Bird's Nest' or the Serpentine Pavilion, and this fact was highly inspiring to us. It inspired us to go beyond just the functional and technical questioning to ask what such a space should actually be. We're very happy that the public function of the stadium in Beijing has been maintained after the Games. For us, the Olympic Games weren't the most important aspect. Of course, they were the trigger to do this building, but we had many different clients because after the Games the building was intended for commercial use. Fortunately this didn't happen. Our third client was the public. Chinese men and women live in the public realm: they dance, they play and they talk together. They're a people who live in public space and we wanted to create more than just a sports facility with this stadium; we wanted to create a public space for the Chinese people and also for their guests in China. The Serpentine Pavilion is similar, since the park is highly public, the Gallery is public and the Pavilion will also be very public. Julia, you mentioned the forum and I think this is a very good word to describe what this Pavilion intends to be: a forum that will bring people together under one roof so that they can meet and exchange ideas. That would certainly be our big hope for the life of this building.

JPJ Do the Olympics give you an additional opportunity, or an additional way of exploring architecture?

AWW Of course, I'm very happy that other people will enjoy the Games, but it doesn't really affect me, because I'm not a very sporty person. Jacques and Pierre are very sporty people. They like playing soccer!

PdM I feel exactly the same as Weiwei. I feel thankful to the Olympic event because it has allowed us to work at the Serpentine Gallery.

HUO Do you have any joint unrealised projects – any Herzog & de Meuron and Ai Weiwei projects that have been too big to be realised, too small to be realised or just forgotten? What are your dreams?

AWW Well it's been a very nice experience spending time and travelling together and I hope we can do it again in the future.

A conversation by Skype
Basel, London, Beijing, 11 May 2012

FOOTPRINTS AND FOUNDATIONS

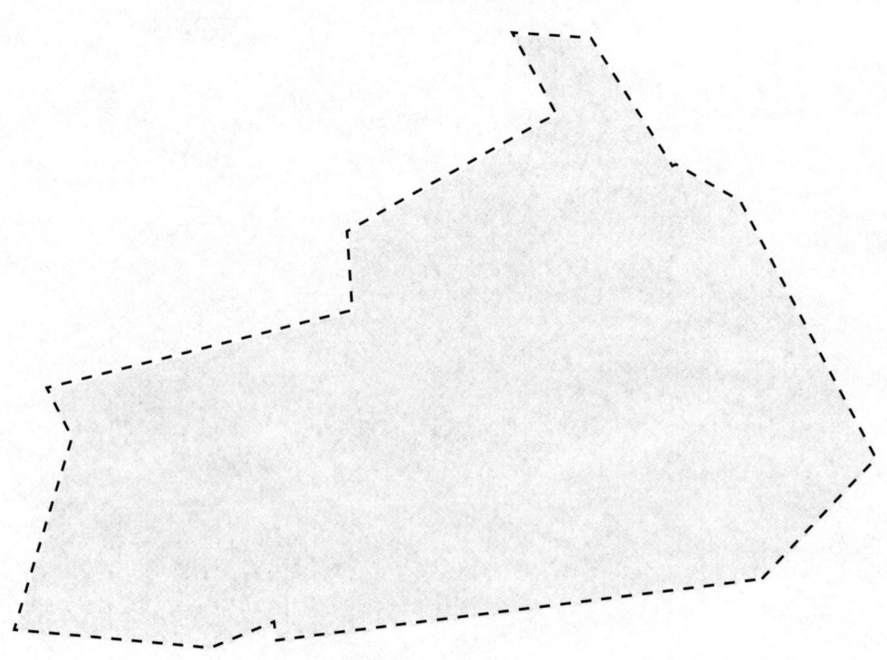

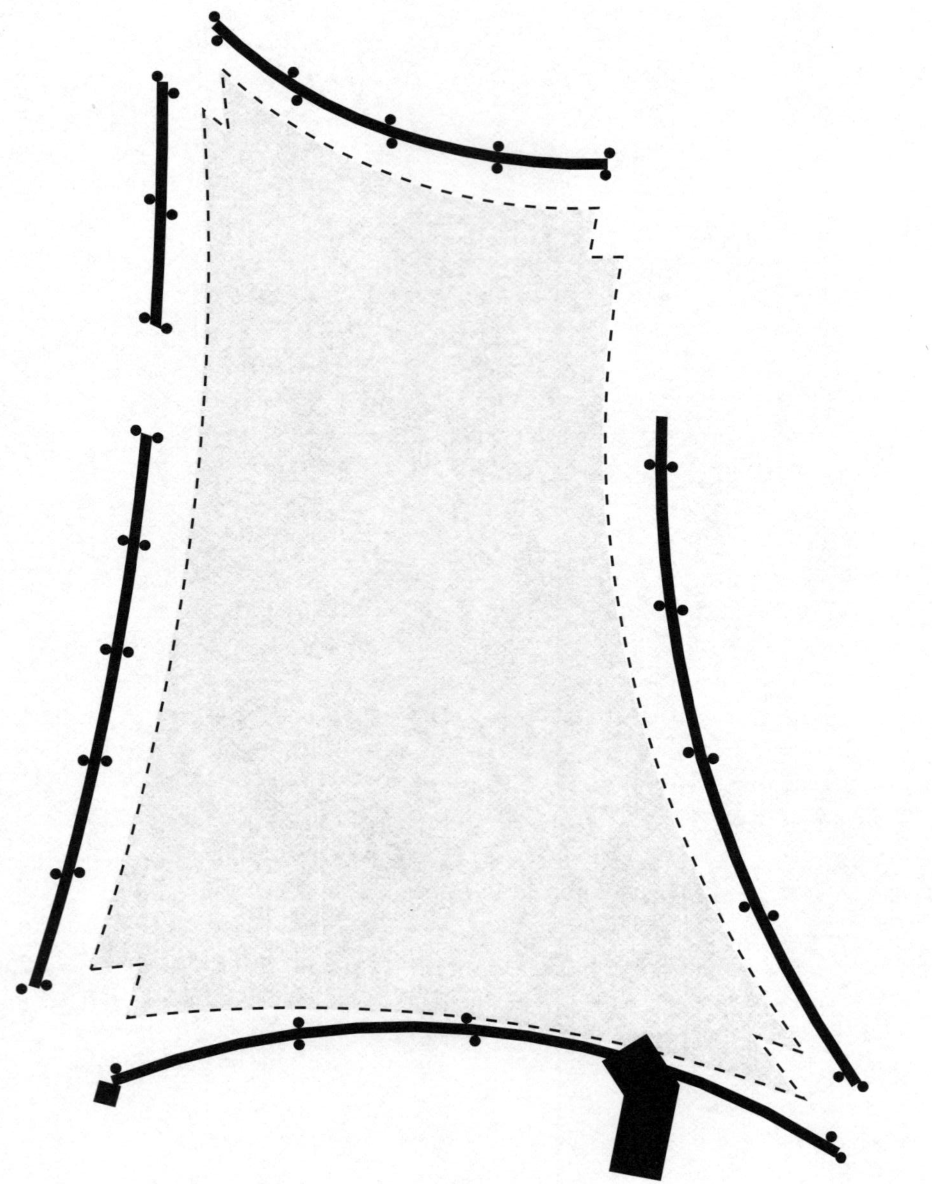

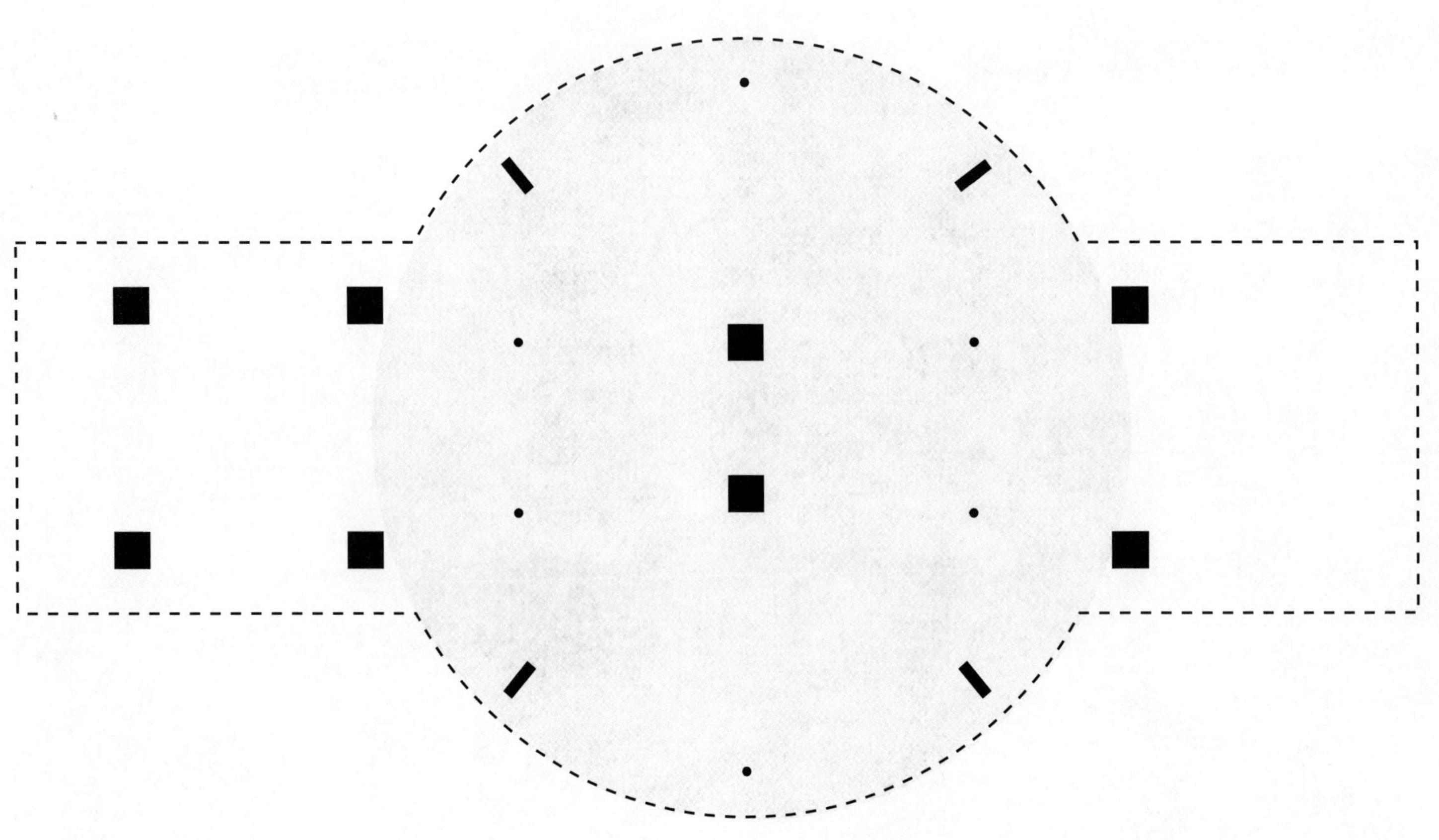

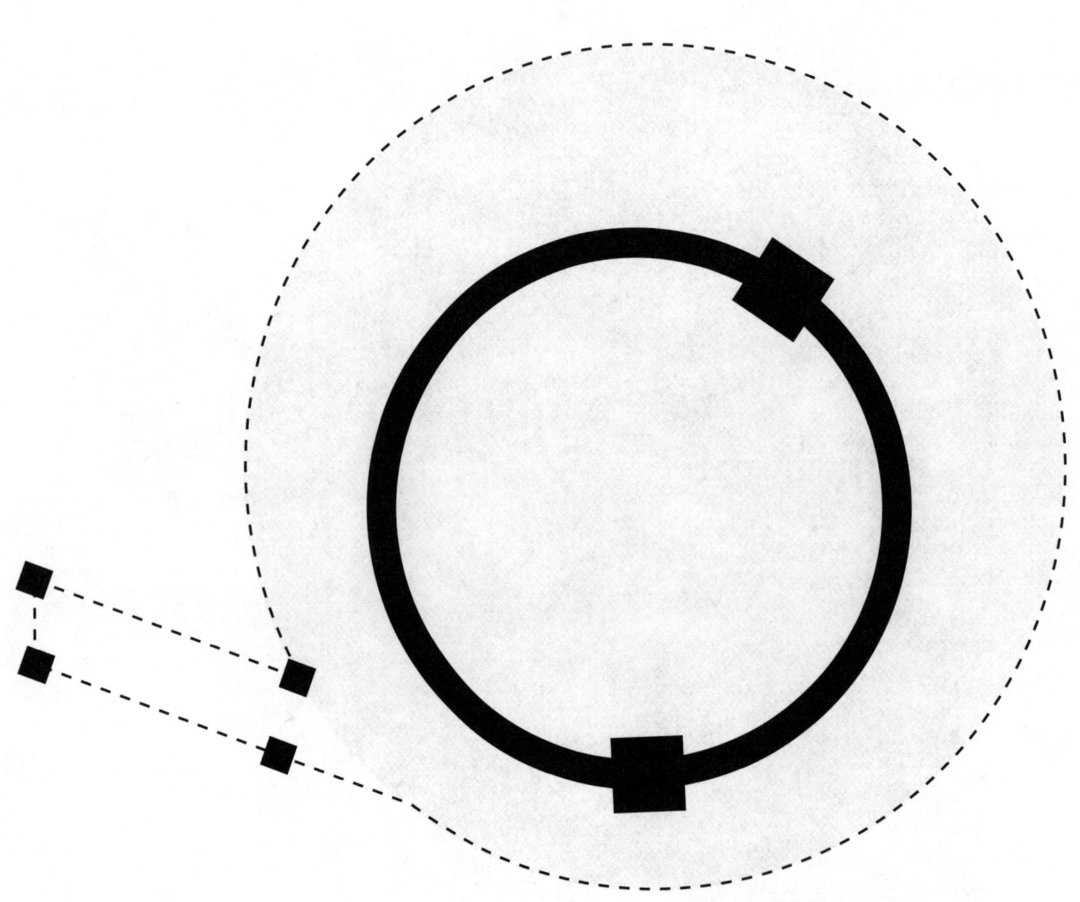

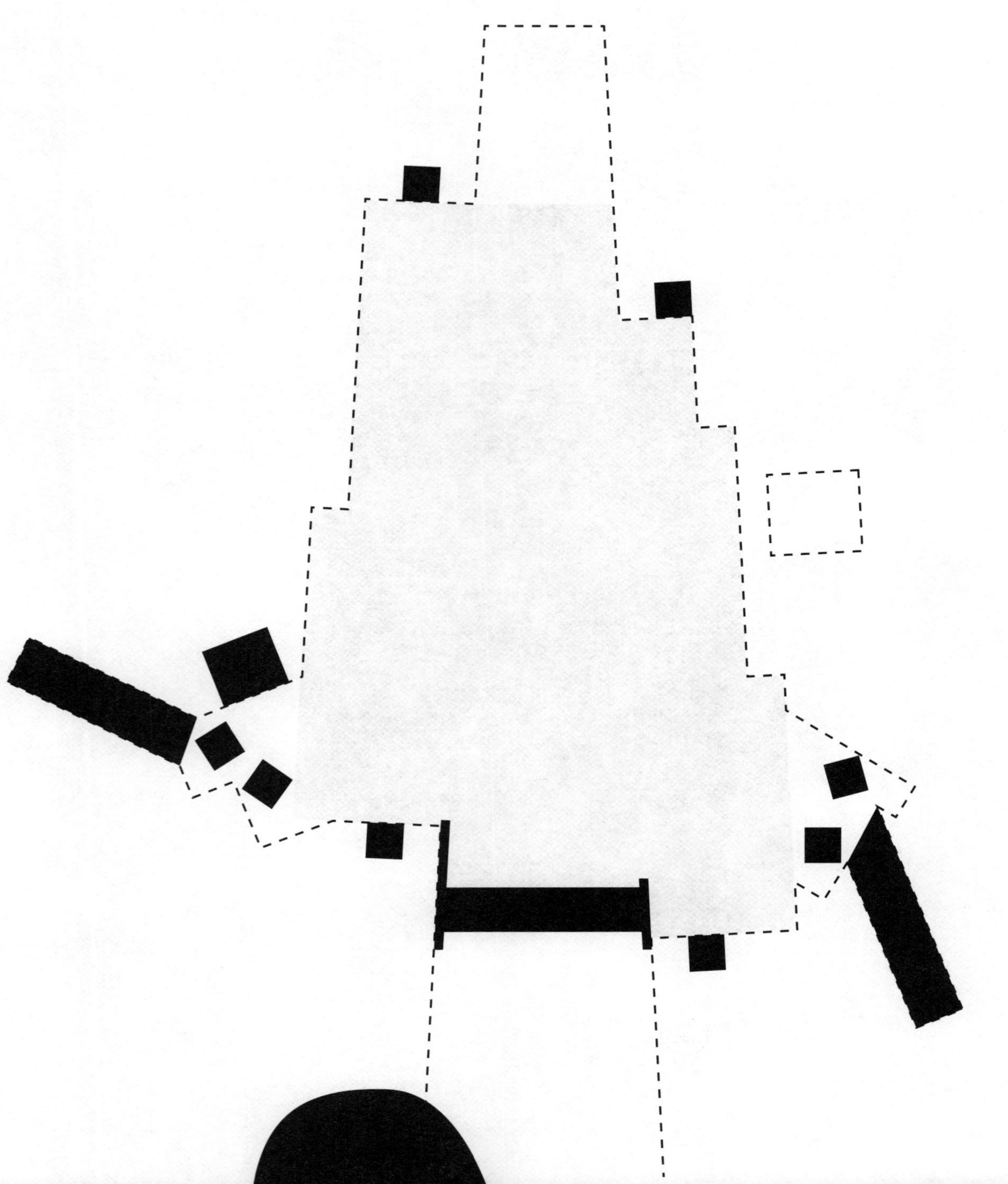

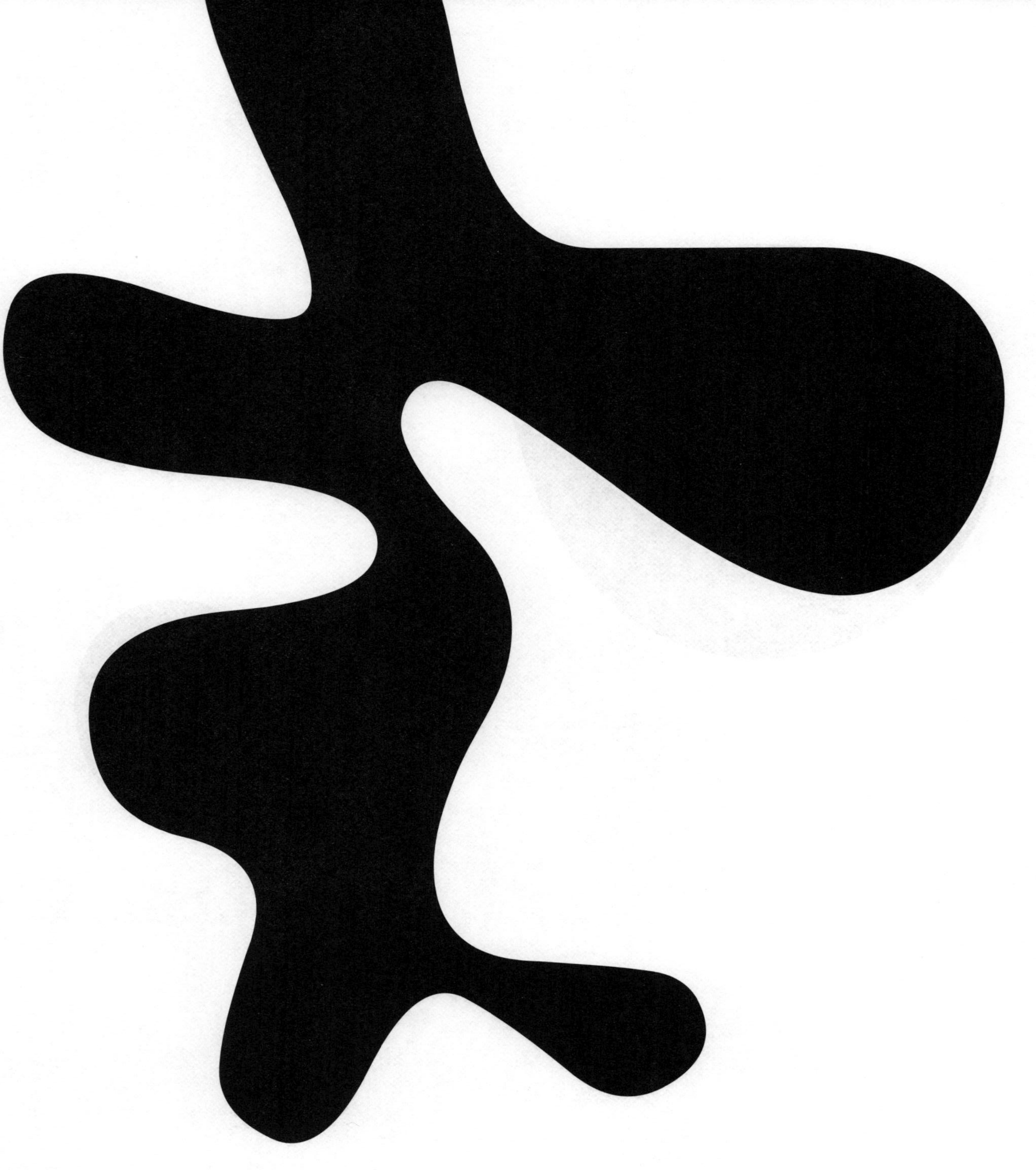

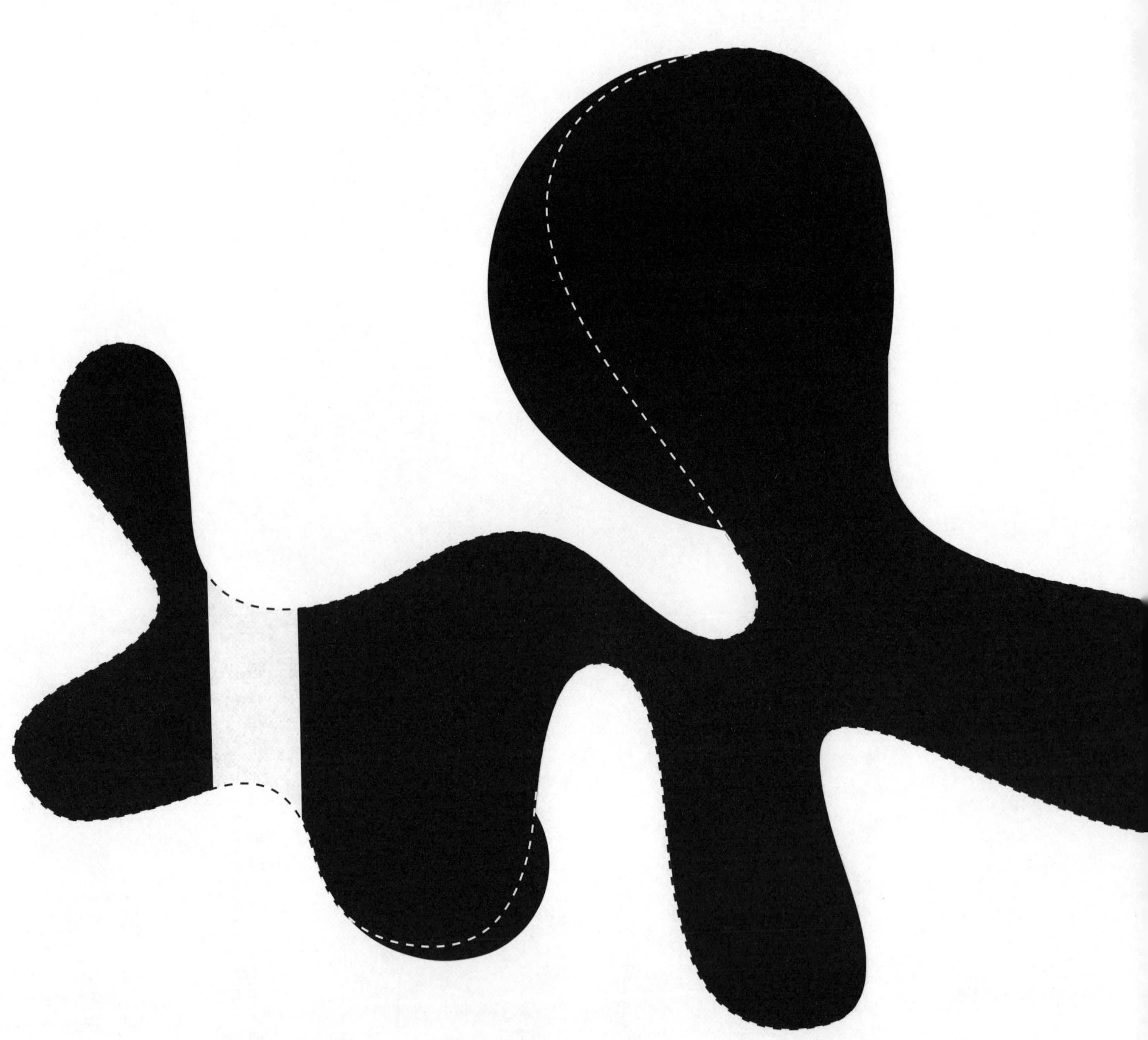

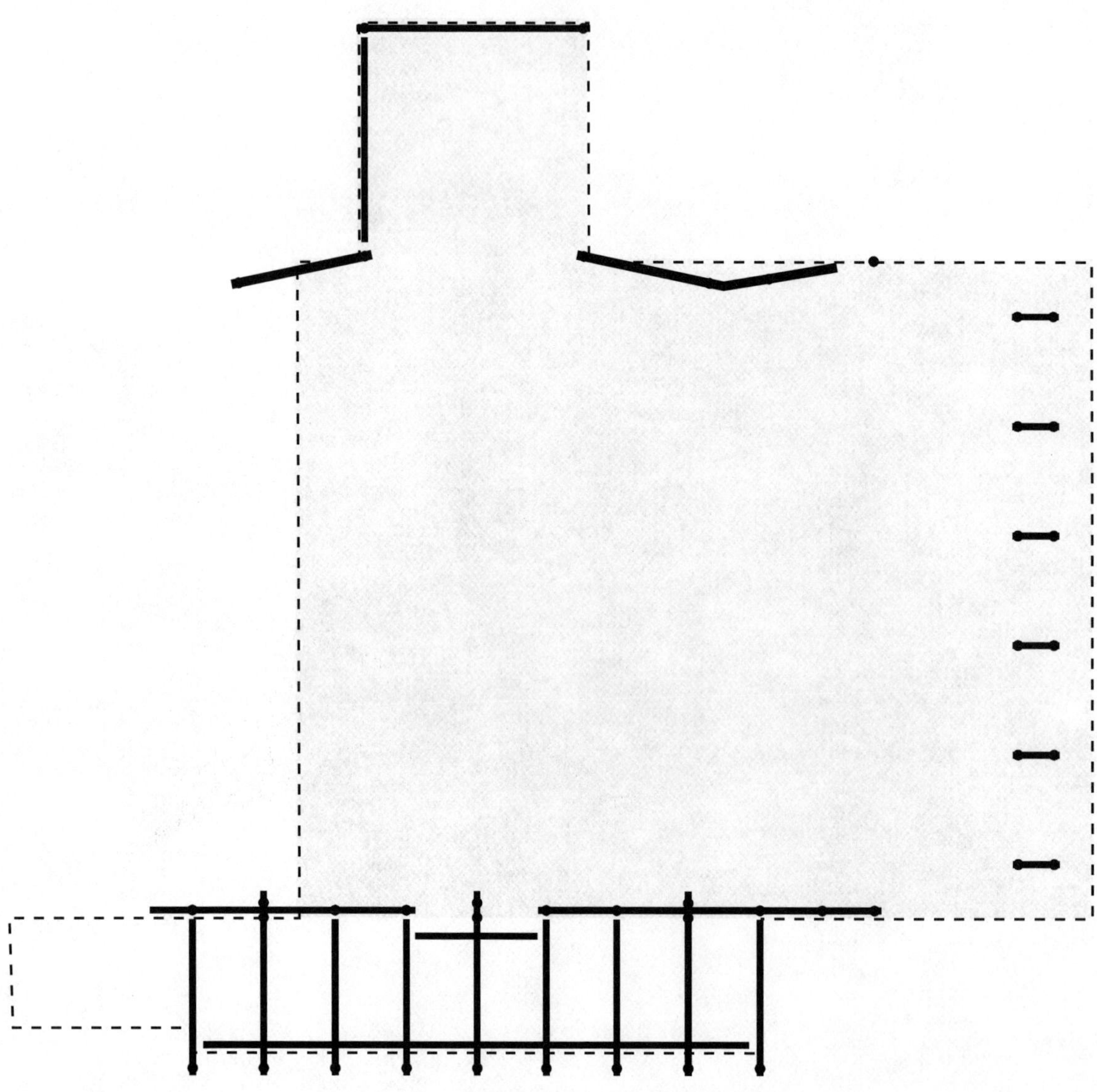

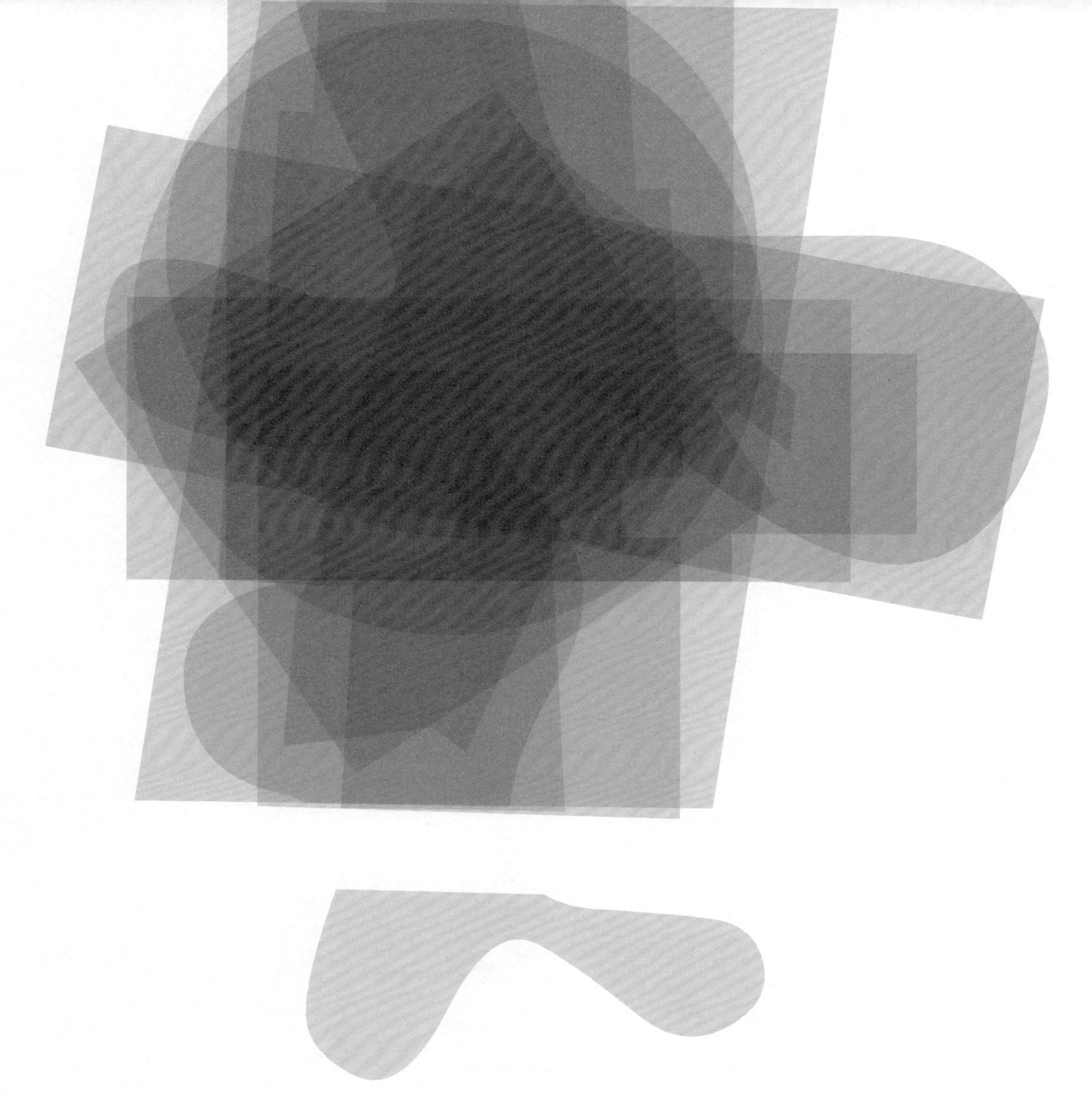

SERPENTINE GALLERY PAVILIONS 2000–2011

Serpentine Gallery Pavilion 2011
Designed by Peter Zumthor (Garden design by Piet Oudolf)

Serpentine Gallery Pavilion 2010
Designed by Jean Nouvel

Serpentine Gallery Pavilion 2009
Designed by Kazuyo Sejima + Ryue Nishizawa/SANAA

Serpentine Gallery Pavilion 2008
Designed by Frank Gehry

Serpentine Gallery Pavilion 2007
Designed by Olafur Eliasson and Kjetil Thorsen

Lilas: an installation by Zaha Hadid Architects 2007
Designed by Zaha Hadid and Patrik Schumacher

Serpentine Gallery Pavilion 2006
Designed by Rem Koolhaas and Cecil Balmond, with Arup

Concept for Serpentine Gallery Pavilion 2004 (unrealised)
Designed by MVRDV with Arup

Serpentine Gallery Pavilion 2002
Designed by Toyo Ito and Cecil Balmond, with Arup

Serpentine Gallery Pavilion 2005
Designed by Álvaro Siza and Eduardo Souto de Moura with Cecil Balmond - Arup

Serpentine Gallery Pavilion 2003
Designed by Oscar Niemeyer

Eighteen Turns, Serpentine Gallery Pavilion 2001
Designed by Daniel Libeskind with Arup

Serpentine Gallery Pavilion 2000
Designed by Zaha Hadid

Biographies

Herzog & de Meuron

Both born in Basel in 1950, Jacques Herzog and Pierre de Meuron studied architecture at the Swiss Federal Institute of Technology Zurich (ETH) from 1970 to 1975 with Aldo Rossi and Dolf Schnebli. They received their degrees in architecture in 1975 and established Herzog & de Meuron in Basel in 1978. Now a partnership led by five Senior Partners, the practice has designed a wide range of projects from the small scale of a private home to the large scale of urban design. The practice has been awarded numerous prizes including the Pritzker Architecture Prize in 2001.

Herzog & de Meuron are known for designs that are at once highly inventive and sensitive to the site, geography and culture of the region for which they are planned. In many projects Herzog & de Meuron have worked with artists, an eminent example of that practice being their collaboration with Ai Weiwei which resulted in the design of three realised projects to date including the Beijing National Stadium (2008).

Jacques Herzog and Pierre de Meuron have been visiting professors at the Harvard Graduate School of Design since 1994. They have been professors at the ETH Zurich since 1999 and co-founded the ETH Studio Basel – Contemporary City Institute in 2002.

Ai Weiwei

Chinese conceptual artist Ai Weiwei also works as an architect, photographer, curator and globally-recognised human rights activist. Born in 1957 in Beijing, he began his training at Beijing Film Academy and later continued at the Parsons School of Design in New York City. His work has been exhibited around the world with one-person exhibitions at Stiftung DKM, Duisburg (2010); Mori Art Museum, Tokyo (2009); Haus der Kunst, Munich (2009); Sherman Contemporary Art Foundation and Cambelltown Arts Centre, Sydney (2008); Groninger Museum, Groningen (2008); and participation in the Venice Biennale in Italy (1999, 2008, 2010); Guangzhou Triennale in China (2002, 2005); Busan Biennial in Korea (2006); Documenta 12 in Germany (2007) and the 29th São Paulo Biennial in Brazil (2010).

In October 2010, Ai Weiwei's *Sunflower Seeds* was installed in the Tate Modern Turbine Hall, London. Ai Weiwei participated in the Serpentine Gallery's *China Power Station* exhibition in 2006, and the *Serpentine Gallery Map Marathon* in 2010.

Serpentine Gallery Pavilion 2012
Project Team

Architects
Herzog & de Meuron
and Ai Weiwei

Architectural Design Team
Jacques Herzog
Pierre de Meuron
Ai Weiwei

Ben Duckworth
(Project Director)
Christoph Zeller
(Project Architect)

Liam Ashmore
Martin Eriksson
Mai Komuro
Martin Nässén
John O'Mara
Wim Walschap
E-Shyh Wong
Inserk Yang

Project Directors
Julia Peyton-Jones
with Hans Ulrich Obrist,
Serpentine Gallery

Project Leader
Julie Burnell,
Serpentine Gallery

Project Organiser
Sophie O'Brien
with Claire Feeley,
Serpentine Gallery

Engineering: Arup
Stuart Smith
Chris Neighbour

Francesco Anselmo
Mark Freeman
Lidia Johnson
Jeff Shaw
Jack Wilshaw

Project and Construction Management: RISE
Gareth Stapleton
Tom Redhouse

Construction: Stage One
Ted Featonby
Mick Mead

Project Advisors
Lord Palumbo, Chairman,
Serpentine Board of Trustees
Paul Lewis, Head of Operations,
Stanhope Plc
Colin Buttery, Director of Parks,
Royal Parks Agency
Ray Brodie, Parks Superintendent,
Royal Parks Agency
Westminster City Council
Planning Office
Jenny Wilson,
Westminster City Council
(Licensing Authority)
Hassan Lashkariani, Westminster
City Council, (Building Control)
London Fire and Emergency
Planning Authority

Consultants
Gleeds (cost management and
contract administrator services)
Knight Frank (assistance
with sale of Pavilion)
Weil, Gotshal & Manges
(legal services)

Contractors
Amorim (cork)
DP9 (planning consultants)
EC Harris (CDM services)
Elliott Thomas Group (site security)
Laing O'Rourke
(construction equipment)
The Landscape Group Ltd
(landscaping)
SES (surveying and site set-out)
Stage One (main structure)

Serpentine Gallery Pavilion 2012 Supporters

Realised with the generous support of

Usha and Lakshmi N. Mittal

Sponsored by

In collaboration with

ESPA

Advisor

ARUP

Platinum Sponsor

rise

Gold Sponsors

Silver Sponsors

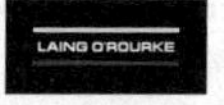

Bronze Sponsors

Pavilion Patrons

LISSON GALLERY

and

GALLERIA CONTINUA, San Gimignano/Beijing/Le Moulin
Lillian and Jon Lovelace
Christophe W. Mao
Oliver Prenn
André Stockamp and Christopher Tsai
Galerie Urs Meile, Beijing-Lucerne
White Rabbit Gallery

Supported by

Supported by ARTS COUNCIL ENGLAND

Art Project powered by Google

swiss arts council prohelvetia

Media Partner

The INDEPENDENT

Serpentine Gallery Acknowledgements

Trustees of the Serpentine Gallery
Lord Palumbo *Chairman*
Felicity Waley-Cohen and Barry Townsley *Co-Vice Chairmen*
Marcus Boyle *Treasurer*
Patricia Bickers
Mark Booth
Roger Bramble
Marco Compagnoni
David Fletcher
Bonnie Greer
Zaha Hadid
Rob Hersov
Colin Tweedy

40th Anniversary Founding Benefactors
Jeanne and William Callanan
The Highmont Foundation
The Luma Foundation

And Founding Benefactors who wish to remain anonymous

Council of the Serpentine Gallery
Rob Hersov *Chairman*
Marlon Abela
Mrs Basil Al-Rahim
Shaikha Paula Al-Sabah
Goga Ashkenazi
Mr and Mrs Harry Blain
Mr and Mrs F. Boglione
Mark and Lauren Booth
Jeanne and William Callanan
Michael Conway and Alison Jacques
Raye Cosbert
Dag Cramér
Alessandro Cajrati Crivelli
Aud and Paolo Cuniberti
Carolyn Dailey
Russ DeLeon and Serge Tiroche
Griet Dupont
Denise Esfandi
Jenifer Evans
Mark Evans
Nicoletta Fiorucci
Lawton W. Fitt and James I. McLaren Foundation
Kathrine and Cecilie Fredriksen
Yakir and Elena Gabay
Ingvild and Stephan Goetz
Olivier de Givenchy
Jonathan Goodwin
Mr and Mrs Lorenzo Grabau
Richard and Odile Grogan
Jennifer and Matthew Harris
Susan and Richard Hayden
Mr and Mrs Tim Jefferies
Mrs Kristi Jernigan
Ella Krasner
Mr and Mrs Jonathan Lourie
The Luma Foundation
Giles Mackay
Leon Max
Pia-Christina Miller
Lakshmi and Usha Mittal
Dalip and Chandrika Pathak
Catherine and Franck Petitgas
Eva Rausing
The Red Mansion Foundation
Yvonne Rieber
Thaddaeus Ropac
Spas and Diliana Roussev
Robin Saunders and Matthew Roeser
Anders and Yukiko Schroeder
David and Simone Sproul
Ahmed and Cherine Tayeb
Robert Tomei
Andrei and Veronika Tretyakov
Andy Valmorbida
Ted Vassilev
Robert and Felicity Waley-Cohen
Bruno Wang
Andrew and Victoria Watkins-Ball
Mr and Mrs Lars Windhorst
Manuela and Iwan Wirth

And members of the Council who wish to remain anonymous

Council's Circle of the Serpentine Gallery
Eric and Sophie Archambeau
Len Blavatnik
Sarah and Ivor Braka
Wayne and Helene Burt
Nicholas Candy
Edwin C. Cohen and The Blessing Way Foundation
Ricki Gail Conway
Guy and Andrea Dellal
Marie Douglas-David
Johan Eliasch
Joey Esfandi
Mala and Oliver Haarmann
The Hon Robert Hanson
Petra and Darko Horvat
Mr and Mrs Michael Hue-Williams
Michael Jacobson
Dakis Joannou
Jolana Leinson and Petri Vainio
Elena Bowes Marano
Jimmy and Becky Mayer
Viviane and James Mayor
Matthew Mellon, in memory of Isabella Blow
Tamara Mellon
Martin and Amanda Newson
J. Harald Orneberg
Stephen and Yana Peel
Silvio and Monica Scaglia
Olivia Schuler-Voith
Mrs Nadja Swarovski-Adams
Phoebe and Bobby Tudor
Hugh Warrender
Beatrice Warrender
Michael Watt
John and Amelia Winter
Michael and Anna Zaoui

And members of the Council's Circle who wish to remain anonymous

Founding Corporate Benefactor
Bloomberg

Exclusive Professional Services Advisor
Deloitte LLP

Platinum Corporate Benefactors
Amorim
Arup
Bloomberg
Diesel
Hiscox
Hugo Boss AG
The Independent
J.P. Morgan Private Bank
LVMH / Moët Hennessy – Louis Vuitton
Maybach
Rise
Weil, Gotshal & Manges

Gold Corporate Benefactors
ESPA
The Kensington Hotel
Laurent-Perrier

Silver Corporate Benefactors
Founders Forum
Gleeds
Laing O'Rourke
The Portman Estate
Stanhope Plc
Vertu

Bronze Corporate Benefactors
agnès b. london endowment fund
Baglioni Hotel
Banco do Brasil
Boujis
By Word of Mouth
The Clerkenwell Kitchen
The Coca-Cola Company
DLD Media GmbH
DP9
EC Harris
Elliott Thomas
The Groucho Club
Knight Frank LLP
The Landscape Group
LMV Design
Maserati
Met Bar at the Metropolitan London
Níall McLaughlin Architects
Perspex Distribution Ltd
Samsung
SCA
Site Engineering Surveys Ltd (SES)
Swiss International Air Lines Ltd
T.Clarke Plc
TAR Magazine

Education Projects supported by
Bloomberg

Education Programme supported by
The Annenberg Foundation
The Baring Foundation
Big Lottery Fund Awards for All
Camden Council
City Bridge Trust
Marie Donnelly
Eranda Foundation
Ernest Cook Trust
David Fawkes and family
The Grocers' Charity
The Haskel Family Foundation
Heritage Lottery Fund
J G Hogg Charitable Trust
Housing Corporation
ICE Futures Charitable Trust
The Kobler Trust
John Lyon's Charity
London Councils
The Mercers' Company
The National Lottery through Arts Council England
The Rayne Foundation
The Dr Mortimer and Theresa Sackler Foundation
The Scotshill Trust
Westminster City Council

And kind assistance from
Old Broad Street Charity Trust
The Philip and Irene Gage Foundation
The Royal Borough of Kensington and Chelsea
Westminster Arts

Exhibition Programme supported by
Marlon Abela, Morton's Club
Charles Asprey
The Colwinston Charitable Trust
Galleria Continua
Galerie Daniel Buchholz, Berlin/Koln
JD & Stuart Evans
Gavin Brown's enterprise
George and Angie Loudon
Barbara Gladstone, New York
Goethe Institut
The Graham Foundation for Advanced Studies in the Fine Arts
Hauser & Wirth Zürich London
The Stanley Thomas Johnson Foundation
Mrs Katrin Henkel
Kunststiftung NRW
The Henry Moore Foundation
Johannes P. Huth
Institut für Auslandsbeziehungen
The Japan Foundation
The Luma Foundation
Lia Rumma Gallery
Lisson Gallery
Lillian and Jon Lovelace
Luhring Augustine, New York
Christophe W. Mao
Matthew Marks, New York
Oliver Prenn
Pro Helvetia
Ramdane Touhami
Ruth and Richard Rogers
Simon Lee Gallery
André Stockamp and Christopher Tsai
The Swiss Cultural Fund in Britain
Galerie Urs Meile, Beijing-Lucerne
White Rabbit Gallery
Zumtobel Group

Learning Council: Committee
Jeanne and Willian Callanan
Gilberto Pozzi
Selina S. Sagayam
Hugh Warrender

Learning Council
Brian and Melinda Carroll
Andrew E Law and Zoe Purvis
Jonathan and Deborah Marks
Eileen and Liad Meidar
Andrew and Jane Partridge
Mark and Elizabeth Thompson
Alta Thorne

Patrons
Marie-Claire, Baroness von Alvensleben
Sofia Barattieri di san Pietro
Ron and Samantha Bauer Charitable Foundation
Colleen De Bonis
Mr and Mrs Charles Bracken
The Hon. Daniel Brennan
The Rory and Elizabeth Brooks Foundation
Mrs Susan Burns
Dr Martin A. Clarke
Sir Ronald and Lady Cohen
Terence and Niki Cole
Alastair Cookson
Grace Contomichalos
Davide Costa
Giulia Costantini
Andrea Dibelius
Frank and Lorna Dunphy
Dr Paul Ettlinger
Christopher Eykyn and Nicholas Maclean
The Edwin Fox Foundation
Mrs Carmen Engelhorn
Fares and Tania Fares
David Fawkes
Adrienne Garrard and Jake Scrivens
Leonardo and Alessia Giangreco
Francesca von Habsburg
The Harman Foundation
Ivana Hasecic and Laurent Cadji
Mrs Katrin Henkel
Yassmin Ghandehari
Karine Giannamore
Francesca Guagnini
Sara Harrison
Jasmine Horowitz
Eva and Iraj Ispahani
Mr and Mrs Karim Juma
Mrs Ghislaine Kane
Tessa Keswick
Ms Audrey Lynn Klein
Martina and Yves Klemmer
Mr and Mrs Simon Lee
Natalie Livingstone
Mr and Mrs J. Jeffry Louis
Andrew and Jacqueline Martin
Jeff and Valerie Montgomery
Mr Donald Moore
Paul and Alison Myners
Sayumi Otake
Joseph and Chloe O'Sullivan
Christina Pamberg
Andrew and Jane Partridge
Alain and Elisabeth Philippe
Mr A.S. Rahman
Mr and Mrs Ivan Ritossa
Kim Samuel-Johnson
Rupert Sanderson
Mr and Mrs Mark Shanker
Siri Stolt-Nielsen
Ian and Mercedes Stoutzker
Laura and Barry Townsley
Rebecca Wang
Helen and Peter Warwick
Welton Foundation
Peter Wheeler and Pascale Revert
Mrs Pauline Witzenfeld
Poju and Anita Zabludowicz

Future Contemporaries Committee
Alia Al-Senussi
Flora Fairbairn
Tim Franks
Rebecca Guinness
Liz Kabler
Dan Macmillan

Bobby Molavi
Jake Parkinson-Smith
Cristina Revert
Andreas Siegfried
Stan Stalnaker
Edward Tang
Christopher Taylor
F. Uribe
Marcus and Alexa Waley-Cohen
Jonathan Wood

Future Contemporaries
Sharifa Alsudairi
Abdullah Alturki
Kamel Alzarka
Mr and Mrs Ben Arbib
Marco Assetto
Flavie Audi
Anja and António Batista
Philip Beatty
Margherita Berloni
Elena Bonanno di Linguaglossa
Ben Bridgewater
James and Felicia Brocklebank
Chris Byrne
William Burlington
May Calil
Louise J Cameron
The Hon. Nicholas Campbell
Antony Clavel and
Maria Novella Vecere
Patrick C. Cunningham
Elizabeth R. DuBois
Roxanna Farboud
Mrs Selma Feriani
Michael Frahm
Hugh Gibson
Marie Guerlain
Michael Hadjedj
Dr Julia and Christoph Hansmeyer
Mr S. Haq
Marine Hartogs
Matt Hermer
Carolyn Hodler
Nicholas W. Hofgren
Jessica Howland
Kamel Jaber
Karim Jallad
Marina Jovanovic
Zoe Karafylakis Sperling
Chloe Kinsman
John Krasner
Niels Kroner
Mans and Abear Larsson
Maged Latif
Kai Lew
James Lindon
Andreas and Elli Loizou
Dan Lywood
Sonia Mak
Jean-David Malat
Marina Marini
Ann-Marie Matthijs
Janna M Miller
John Paul Micalleff
Laura Modiano
Fernando J. Moncho Lobo
Sheryl Needham
Isabelle Nowak and Torsten Winkler
David Eric Olsson

Sophie Orde
Jake and Samira Parkinson-Smith
Anja Pauls
Joe Phelon
Carlos and Francesca Pinto
Mike Radcliffe
Piotr Rejmer
Claudia Ruimy
Poppy Sebire
Xandi Schemann
Henrietta Shields
Andy Simmons
Tammy Smulders
Isadora Mercereau Tharin
Andy Valmorbida
Rachel Verghis
Sam Waley-Cohen
Trent Ward
Hillary Webb
Jonathan and Lucy Wood
Mr and Mrs Nabil Zaouk
Fabrizio D. Zappaterra

Benefactors
Mr and Mrs Allahyar Afshar
Cosima and Clemens Aichholzer
Shane Akeroyd
Paul and Kia Armstrong
Jane Attias
Anne Best and Roddy
Kinkead-Weekes
Mr and Mrs John Botts
Marcus Boyle
Mervyn and Helen Bradlow
Vanessa Branson
Benjamin Brown
Ed Burstell
Mrs Tita Granda Byrne
Lavinia Calza Beveridge
Sadie Coles
Carole and Neville Conrad
Matthew Conrad
Gul Coskun
Yasmine Datnow
Mr and Mrs Colin David
Mr and Mrs Christopher Didizian
Mike Fairbrass
Mr and Mrs Mark Fenwick
Heidi Ferid-Hands
John Ferreira
Hako and Dörte, Graf and Gräfin
von Finckenstein
David and Jane Fletcher
Jane and Richard Found
Eric and Louise Franck
Alan and Joanna Gemes
David Gill
Dimitri J. Goulandris
Richard and Judith Greer
Linda and Richard Grosse
Louise Hallett
Liz Hammond
Jeremy Hargreave
Susan Harris
Timothy and Daška Hatton
Maria and Stratis Hatzistefanis
Alison Henry-Davies
Mrs Christine Johnston
Marcelle Joseph and Paolo Cicchiné
Jennifer Kersis

James and Clare Kirkman
Mr and Mrs Lahoud
Geraldine Larkin
Julie Lee
Anne and Sydney Levinson
George and Angie Loudon
Mr Otto Julius Maier and
Mrs Michèle Claudel-Maier
Cary J. Martin
Penny Mather
Ruth and Robert Maxted
Viviane and James Mayor
Warren and Victoria Miro
Dr Maigaelle Moulene
Paul Munford
Georgia Oetker
Jacqueline O'Leary
Desmond Page and Asun Gelardin
Maureen Paley
Dominic Palfreyman
Midge and Simon Palley
Julia Peyton-Jones OBE
Sophie Price
Mathew Prichard
Mrs Janaki Prosdocimi
Ashraf Qizilbash
Bruce and Shadi Ritchie
Kimberley Robson-Ortiz
Jacqueline and Nicholas Roe
Fabio Rossi
Victoria, Lady de Rothschild
James Roundell and Bona Montagu
Michael and Julia Samuel
Joana and Henrik Schliemann
Nick Simou and Julie Gatland
Bina and Philippe von Stauffenberg
Simone and Robert Suss
The Thames Wharf Charity
Britt Tidelius
Gretchen and Jus Trusted
Audrey Wallrock
Lady Corinne Wellesley
Alannah Weston
Helen Ytuarte White
Dr Yvonne Winkler
Mr Ulf Wissen
Henry and Rachel Wyndham
Mr and Mrs Nabil Zaouk

And Learning Council, Patrons,
Future Contemporaries
and Benefactors who wish
to remain anonymous

Supported by
Arts Council England
The Royal Parks
Westminster City Council

Staff of the Serpentine Gallery

Directors

Director, Serpentine Gallery & Co-Director, Exhibitions & Programmes
Julia Peyton-Jones

Co-Director, Exhibitions & Programmes & Director of International Projects
Hans Ulrich Obrist

Chief Operating Officer
Jackie McNerney

Executive Assistant to Julia Peyton-Jones
Katie Doubleday

Junior PA to Hans Ulrich Obrist
Alicia Harrop

Research Assistant to Julia Peyton-Jones
Poppy Parry

Personal Assistant to Julia Peyton-Jones
Jennifer Taylor

Executive Assistant to Hans Ulrich Obrist
Lorraine Two

Buildings

Head of Projects
Julie Burnell

Duty Managers
Katherine Kiorgaard
René Songui

PA to Head of Projects
Amy Fraser

Junior PA to Head of Projects
Clare Hallin

Commerce

Head of Commerce
Gregory Krum

Communications

Head of Communications
Rose Dempsey

Head of Press
Tom Coupe

Web Editor
William Barrett

Communications Print Manager
Mary Lehner

Communications Co-ordinator
Varind Ramful

Development & Events

Head of Campaigns
Louise McKinney

Head of Fundraising
Sarah Robinson

Head of Events
Michelle Anselmo

Trusts and Foundations Co-ordinator
Victoria Foord

Editions and Information Manager
Tom Harrisson

PA to Head of Fundraising
Sam Hazelden

Corporate Development Co-ordinator
Charlie Hill

Head of Corporate Development
Katherine Holmgren

Prints Assistant
Matthew Johnstone

Individual Giving Manager
Arianne Lovelace

Head of Grants, Trusts and Foundations
Lee Rodwell

Membership Manager, Individual Giving
Rachel Stephens

Researcher
Sydney Townsend

Events Organiser
Duncan Welsh

Finance

Financial Accountant
Vanessa Teixeira

Finance Assistant
Annand Wiffen

Human Resources

Interim Head of Human Resources
Gwen Barry

HR Assistant
Claire Vernazza

Programmes

Assistant Curator
Claire Feeley

Gallery Manager
Mike Gaughan

Assistant Gallery Manager
Matt Glenn

Projects Curator
Janna Graham

Education Curator
Joceline Howe

Assistant Curator, Projects
Amal Khalaf

Senior Public Programmes Curator
Nicola Lees

Assistant Curator
Rebecca Lewin

Senior Exhibition Curator
Sophie O'Brien

Assistant Curator, Public Programmes
Lucia Pietroiusti

Senior Exhibition Curator
Kathryn Rattee

Gallery Assistants

Senior Gallery Assistants
Anna Curtis
Hannah Lees
Mary Toal
Rosalind Inett
Nathan Williams

Gallery Assistants
Mark Dillon
Aida Dolrahim
Stephen Draycott
Sarah Ormond
Michael Pybus
Joana Roberto
Jo Savill
Phil Thompson
Helen Wood

This catalogue is published to accompany the Serpentine Gallery Pavilion 2012 designed by Herzog & de Meuron and Ai Weiwei, 1 June – 14 October 2012.

Publication concept by Herzog & de Meuron and Ai Weiwei: Jacques Herzog, Pierre de Meuron, Ai Weiwei, Donald Mak, Aliénor de Chambrier, Esther Zumsteg

Editors Sophie O'Brien, with Melissa Larner and Claire Feeley
Design Irma Boom Office
Publication advisor Karen Marta
Transcription Rebecca Catt
Translation Catherine Schelbert (German to English, page 50)

Production Printmanagement Plitt, Oberhausen
Printed in Germany

ISBN: 978-3-86335-220-2
Koenig Books, London

ISBN: 978-1-908617-07-1
Serpentine Gallery, London

The Serpentine Gallery is supported by

THE ROYAL PARKS

Serpentine Gallery

Serpentine Gallery
Kensington Gardens
London W2 3XA
t +44 (0)20 7402 6075
f +44 (0)20 7402 4103
www.serpentinegallery.org

First published by Koenig Books, London, and the Serpentine Gallery, London

Koenig Books Ltd
At the Serpentine Gallery
Kensington Gardens
London W2 3XA
www.koenigbooks.co.uk

Distribution

Buchhandlung Walther König, Köln
Ehrenstr. 4, 50672 Köln
t +49 (0) 221 / 20 59 6 – 53
f +49 (0) 221 / 20 59 6 – 60
verlag@buchhandlung-walther-koenig.de

Switzerland
AVA Verlagsauslieferungen AG
Centralweg 16
CH-8910 Affoltern a.A.
Tel. +41 (44) 762 42 60
Fax +41 (44) 762 42 10
verlagsservice@ava.ch

UK & Eire
Cornerhouse Publications
70 Oxford Street
Manchester M1 5NH
t +44 (0) 161 200 15 03
f +44 (0) 161 200 15 04
publications@cornerhouse.org

Outside Europe
D.A.P. / Distributed Art Publishers, Inc.
155 6th Avenue, 2nd Floor
USA-New York, NY 10013
Fon +1 (0) 212 627 1999
Fax +1 (0) 212 627 9484
eleshowitz@dapinc.com